How Wide the Heart

How Wide the Heart

The Roots of Peace in Palestine and Israel

Marko Pogačnik
Ana Pogačnik

Translated by Catherine E. Creeger

Lindisfarne Books

First published in German as *Das Herz so weit: Zu den Wurzeln des Friedens in Palastina und Israel* by Atmospharen Verlag, Munchen, 2004.

All of the photographs were taken by Ana Pogačnik. The maps on pages 192–193 were drawn by Astrid Fischer-Leitl, Munich.

Published by Lindisfarne Books
610 Main Street
Great Barrington, MA 01230

www.lindisfarne.org

Library of Congress Cataloging-in-Publication Data

Pogačnik, Marko, 1944-
[Herz So Weit. English]
How wide the heart : the roots of peace in Palestine and Israel / Marko, Ana Pogačnik ; translated by Catherine E. Creeger.
p. cm.
ISBN 1-58420-039-1
1. Arab-Israeli conflict—1993—Peace—Miscellanea. 2. Geomancy. 3. Meditations. I. Pogačnik, Ana. II. Title.
DS119.76.P6413 2006
133.3'33—dc22

2006014830

Contents

Part II / Ana Pogačnik

For our dear friend Peter Vieweger,
who birthed the name and soul of this book:
"We were so close to his heart that he lives on in us."

Foreword to the American Edition

The book you hold in your hands was not written primarily to explain the situation in Israel/Palestine. We tried to create it in such a way that the book could work as a tool in changing the present hopeless situation in the Holy Land.

But can a book at all serve as a practical tool in the work for peace and justice?

To secure a vivid interaction between the message of the book and the situation in Israel/Palestine, we implemented several methods:

- The text that Ana received through inspiration carries within the capability to establish an energy flow that can clarify the religious, personal, and cultural relationships involved in the conflict around Israel/Palestine.
- Through the proposed cycle of seven meditations, it is possible to work on seven aspects of the peace process in Israel/Palestine, by working on one's own energy and emotional fields.
- A number of cosmograms were created, to stimulate some of the most important vital-energy centers of the Near East.
- The work toward a lasting peace envisioned through this book is being carried out by the authors with local groups within the energy field of Israel/Palestine.

The present book has possibilities to offer for everyone, to engage in the conflict resolution in a country that has the unique capability to reflect the world situation–in good and in bad. Let us together work for the good!

Šempas and Munich, March 23, 2006

Ana Pogačnik
Marko Pogačnik

Introduction

To many of us, it is almost inconceivable that we human beings are capable of violence and mutual contempt, yet they manifest every day before our very eyes, and unfortunately with extra intensity and potency in the country the West calls the "Holy Land."

Our desire to learn about this country in greater depth—that is, to understand the causes and background of the conflict smoldering there—and the impulse to seek ways of achieving a lasting peace inspired a trip that grew out of the inner vision of our friend Gabriele Ulich of Berlin and took place around Easter 2001. The participants were a group of people interested in geomancy and peace-making.

The archetypal route from the Pyramids across the Sinai Peninsula to Jerusalem led us past many of the holy places of three world religions (Judaism, Islam, and Christianity). Immersing ourselves in the essence of these sites also enabled us to decipher their vital-energetic, emotional, and spiritual dimensions. Tuning in to the locations and landscapes of several acupuncture points in the Near East resulted in personal experiences that sowed the seeds of regenerative impulses. Throughout our trip, we were fascinated by the country's human diversity and the beauty of its landscape. Nonetheless, the book you are holding in your hands is no travelogue.

In addition to profound personal experiences, the forces or aspects of the landscape that we felt privileged to encounter (and especially the interference between them) inspired one participant, publisher Peter Vieweger, to suggest compiling a collective journal by all the participants. He dedicated himself enthusiastically to this project and put a great deal of energy and attention into reading all of our reports, notes, rough drafts, and ideas with the intention of compiling them into a single text. When Peter crossed the threshold, the driving force behind the original impulse was lost and with it the possibility of pursuing the project as he had envisioned it.

When a new publisher supplied a new concept based on two main texts, the actual physical journey and the participants' reports retreated into the background and began to serve simply as the context for the book's actual contents. After multiple attempts to incorporate all our reports into the book in journal fashion, several things became clear: the trip had left behind many important impulses in us participants; our common experiences had sparked points of light in all our lives; we had left traces of healing behind us in the landscapes we passed through. Nonetheless, the trip itself, as an accomplished fact, already seemed so distant that it would have been difficult to compile our impressions effectively. It would also have been a shame to pin down such a unique and spontaneous experience.

In the end, a different book emerged. In it, the subject of the trip itself is subsumed in a holistic view of the planetary role and true identity of the Near East. In Part I, Marko translates our experiences of individual places en route to the insights and concepts that made this view possible and revealed the energy needed to access these places appropriately.

"Appropriate access" is the portal that allows us to approach the essence of a place or landscape directly. An appropriate angle of approach avoids obstacles concealing the essential aspects of the place. In Marko's experience, the "portal" to Israel/Palestine is the archetypal route from Egypt across the Sinai Peninsula toward Jerusalem, the route first taken by the Israelites under the leadership of Moses and his brother Aaron. If we tune in to modern, holistic consciousness, this ancient route proves to be an inspiring opportunity to approach the geomantic and social layers that will ultimately allow peace to take root in Israel/Palestine.

During our original trip in 2001, we made an effort to involve local people in our activity because we already knew that an impulse for peace can bear fruit only if supported from within and not merely transplanted from outside. In Sekem and Kiryat Tivon, we gave talks on the motivation for our trip and invited anyone interested to participate in our geomantic explorations of the Golan Heights and Jerusalem. In subsequent years, Marko conducted three Earth Healing workshops for Israelis, one in Jerusalem and around Mount Carmel (2002), one in the area around the Sea of Galilee (2004), and one in the Dead Sea area (2006).

Marko's experiences served as the basis of two new projects to promote peace in Israel/Palestine. These projects, which round out Part 1 of this book, will also allow you, our readers, to contribute individually to the collective search for peace in the Near East. The first project is a weekly cycle of seven meditations to promote peace both within the individual and in Israel/Palestine. It can be implemented in any given week but should always be started on a Sunday; meditations for each day of the week follow. The second project involves eight cosmograms developed by Marko to support the places of healing in the geographical area between the Pyramids, Sinai, and

Jerusalem. These cosmograms actively embody the vital-energetic and spiritual foundations of the transformation that will turn the present waves of destruction into impulses for peace. We hope that you, our readers, will feel called upon to photocopy these cosmograms or reproduce them in artistic media of your choice and to find places to post them.

In Part II, there is no longer any direct connection to our original trip in 2001. This half of the book contains the messages Ana received last year from the deep source of love and wisdom that we in the West call Christ energy. Ana's text functions on several levels simultaneously. One level addresses us individually, calling on us to look more closely at our own life and to follow our chosen path with increased consciousness and equanimity. On another level, it takes life, lifestyles, the heart's energy, and the power of the Christ to a universal level and shows them from a different perspective. A parallel level describes the process humankind has undergone in the course of history and reveals important moments in this process—moments that determined our common path, thus providing impulses for evolution as a whole.

A "red thread" running through all of these messages is our connection to our religions and the interferences, complexities, and friction that result, as well as the danger that arises when we do not approach this connection as independent individuals.

A subsequent section describes how life-energy is anchored in a specific energetic structure in the landscape around the Sea of Galilee, revealing the important role played and reflected by this area. This description reestablishes the bridge to the landscape as such, which is central to the book as a whole.

In conclusion, self-reflection reveals that if peace is to be achieved on earth, it can and should develop within us first. In this way, each of us has a great deal to contribute to this healing process.

The photos in this book were taken by Ana during our trip in 2001. We hope they will allow your hearts to experience at least a little of the flavor of the Near East.

In conclusion, we would like to thank Gabriele Ulich for the crucial initial impulse for the trip of 2001. We would also like to thank all who helped to shape the trip and participated in it, because our experiences with that group of people formed the basis for this book. Heartfelt thanks to all who wrote contributions for the book as it was originally conceived, and especially to Margit Holland for her considerable efforts in compiling participants' journals. We would also especially like to thank Stefan Stawicki-Seifert for his supportive advice and help during the conceptual design of the book.

Oberweningen, April 26, 2004
Ana Pogačnik and Marko Pogačnik

Part I

Marko Pogačnik

From the Pyramids across Sinai toward Jerusalem: The Route of Reconnection

Introduction

At the very outset, we are confronted with a question: When a country is suffering so intensely, do we even have the right to attempt to perceive it in a way that transcends the seemingly endless political conflicts and dramatic social breakdowns that are occurring there? Ultimately, independent perception also means being privileged to pay attention to levels of existence that appear unrelated to sorely needed solutions to the conflict. Essential insights may lie concealed in levels of existence that are completely masked by daily reports of violence and disasters. Raised to consciousness and implemented in practice, these insights might contribute to a lasting solution of the overall problem.

We are well aware that a new "Berlin Wall" is now being constructed in Israel/Palestine and that individuals on both sides of this dividing wall are being subjected to suffering and almost unbearable hopelessness. On the other hand, we also know from our own experience that states of suffering and hopelessness commonly appear in the everyday lives of individuals facing decisive transformations. When we confront the prospect of radical change, we suddenly encounter completely unprecedented difficulties in our lives. Gradually, however, we learn to interpret these unfortunate circumstances without regard for their threatening appearance and to recognize them as "soul words" that are attempting to tell us that it is time to bid farewell to certain ideas, goals, or patterns of behavior. An epoch of transformation is dawning in full force! It's time to open our inner world to completely new, audacious, as yet undreamed-of intuitions and thoughts. As we gradually integrate them into our life, they will fundamentally change our personal reality.

Is it also possible for an entire country to be pulled into the confusion of such a transformation? Can a previously unrecognized aspect of its wholeness appear step by step as a result? If so, conflicts and breakdowns must serve to shatter old structures holding the country captive in its rigid past and thus to create a free space where the new can be revealed. This might indeed apply to Israel/Palestine, that country of two names that forces its way into our consciousness on an almost daily basis with its tragic news.

This same country was once the setting for divine revelation. Three thousand years ago, the covenant between the Jews and their God left a decisive imprint on the West's relationship to life as a whole. The Islamic tradition, too, finds a foundation of its faith here, and the Christ's incarnation and the revelation of his love and healing energy also took place here. The four Gospels that report the activity and teachings of Jesus Christ served as the basis for the development of Western culture. For millions of people throughout the world, these Gospels still constitute a source of inspiration in religious and artistic, social and interpersonal domains.

Let's assume that the shattering juxtaposition of divine revelation and armed conflict in Israel/Palestine is a sign of impending transformation. We must keep in mind that the relentless wars in this country are not a phenomenon of recent decades but have been going on for centuries. But whose intentions are secretly at work here?

When transformations occur in the life of an individual, the underlying intentions can usually be found in that person's eternal soul. The soul (the individual's cosmic "I," which transcends spatial and temporal constraints) intervenes on behalf of the person's forgotten inner gifts and qualities. Once the cosmic moment of their revelation dawns in that person's life, the soul induces circumstances that herald an epoch of transformation. The storm begins to gather.

Can a comparable cosmic consciousness with the desire to introduce specific change also exist within a landscape? In such instances, holistic ecological research—geomancy—speaks of the "soul layer," "Goddess," or quintessence of a country. To explain more precisely what we mean by these terms, let's relate this quintessence to the integrated *gestalt* of the human being. One of the fundamental ideas of modern geomancy is that the human being is a holographic fragment of the Earth or of the landscape. Conversely, considering the human constitution leads us to conclude that landscapes also consist of multiple layers.

To keep the multidimensionality of human beings and landscapes as simple as possible, we can merge their many different layers into four fundamental dimensions: life-energy, consciousness, the materialized body, and the eternal soul.

- LIFE-ENERGY: We would not be living human beings if our bodies were not pervaded by the flow of life-energy. Similarly, from the perspective of geomancy, a breathing, fruitful landscape exists only because it is enlivened by a "body" of life forces. This body consists of energy lines (ley lines of various types), force centers (earth chakras), and energy fields. This is the vital-energetic (or etheric or bioenergetic) layer, which maintains and nourishes the living quality of both landscapes and human beings.
- CONSCIOUSNESS: A human being without consciousness is inconceivable. The same is true of the natural world, of both landscapes and the Earth as a whole. Almost all aboriginal traditions agree that thought-energy is incorporated into the earthly world by elemental beings, fairies, or nature spirits. In this context, we speak of an integrated consciousness-field that pervades all living things and enables them to communicate. Thus fairies, nymphs, tree spirits, landscape devas (or whatever else we choose to call them) represent different functions within the overall consciousness of nature or the Earth. Of course we humans are also integrally involved in this holistic consciousness.
- THE MATERIALIZED BODY: The relationship between the materialized body of a landscape and the human body is probably the easiest of these connections to describe. The human skeleton corresponds to the landscape's geological formations, carved out of layers of stone. Our circulating blood can be compared to the "veins" of rivers, our skin to the thin layer of fertile soil, etc.
- THE ETERNAL SOUL: In contrast to the materialized body, the soul layer is relatively free of spatial and temporal constraints. An individual's quintessential soul exists before birth and after death as well as in the time between birth and death. Actually, the quintessential soul is the individual. If we were to equate a human individual with his or her soul, only the earthly garment would be lacking. All other aspects of that individual—archetypal identity, knowledge of the meaning of life, stored memories, and the power of love—belong to the microcosm of the soul.

Everything that applies to the human soul also applies to a landscape's soul-essence. The human soul corresponds to a country's unique identity, which develops through eons as a result of the vibrations of nature's consciousness in that area in interaction with the consciousness of the Earth as a whole. Relatively free of the constraints of space and time, the landscape-soul guards the knowledge of its country's fundamental qualities and of its role within the totality of the earthly cosmos. In this sense, the soul of a country remains somewhat aloof from the momentary activity of the local culture within "its" landscape.

This does not mean, however, that there is no communication between the landscape-soul and local culture. The pure essence of creation that gives rise to the culture in question is integrated into and enriches the archetypal pattern of the landscape. Conversely, the soul—or the "Goddess" of the landscape—attempts to stimulate certain events in the local culture with the intention of enhancing that culture's sensitivity to hidden qualities of the land.

When tenacious prejudices or collective fears or blockages counteract the revelation of specific qualities of the land, the soul initiates specific transformative processes. The resulting political, social, and cultural revolutions may be profoundly painful for local cultures (in this case, for Palestinians and Israelis), but they are relatively simple to dissolve. Peace would immediately supplant war if the original intention leading to the transformative process were recognized.

We have just described the fundamental hope that inspired a group of twenty-nine individuals, primarily from German-speaking countries, to undertake a pilgrimage in 2001. Our journey led first from the Giza plateau (the site of the Sphinx and the Pyramids) across the Sinai Peninsula to the shores of the Red Sea. From there, we followed the Jordan rift valley to the Sea of Galilee and then swung back to Jerusalem.

Following the Archetypal Route of Transformation

Undeniably, our route was inspired by the Jews' celebrated exodus from Egyptian captivity under the leadership (according to biblical accounts) of Moses and his brother Aaron. Legend tells us how the Jewish people were freed from bondage in Egypt and set out on their fateful migration across the Sinai Peninsula to Israel/Palestine. The point of our pilgrimage, however, was not to retrace the biblical wanderings of the Jews in search of the Promised Land. By no means. Rather, its character was meant to be determined by a contemporary energy and message. Our pilgrimage merely alluded to the three stages of the biblical exodus, in which the three settings of Egypt, Sinai, and Israel/Palestine played specific roles.

- EGYPT stands for misery, death, and misfortune. As the Bible reports, a series of plagues fell on the Egyptian countryside. The water of the Nile turned to blood, so all the fish died. Frogs overwhelmed the land, followed by boils and other infestations. Thunder and lightning proclaimed the dawn of the epoch of transformation.

- SINAI represents the phase of transformation when the old must be let go in order to forge a connection to the new. The traditional ritual of honoring the divine, "worshipping the golden calf," was cursed and the Israelites entered into a new type of covenant with their God. On Mount Sinai, Moses received the Ten Commandments as guidelines for developing a new, monotheistic culture fundamentally different in character from the cultures of the past.
- ISRAEL/PALESTINE, in the context of the biblical migration, is depicted as the Promised Land where milk and honey flow. This land was promised a very specific spiritual task in the future—in the symbolic language of the Bible, the Jewish people would be "appointed to an everlasting priesthood." Israel/Palestine, the so-called Holy Land, stands for the actualization of what began in the Sinai desert and later found expression in Jewish culture.

If we extract the three stages of the migration from Egypt across Sinai to Israel/Palestine from their historical context, it is not difficult to overlook the fact that they represent an archetypal pattern of transformation of universal importance not only to human individuals but in the evolution of humankind as a whole:

- PHASE ONE: The time of transformation is presaged by occasional incidents and breakdowns. Social and cultural systems experience repeated crises. Old patterns of existence become outdated as spiritual evolution continues; they decline and die. Here and there, new ideas and inspirations flare up and disappear again, comet-like, in the general mood of mourning and doom.
- PHASE TWO is characterized by the unveiling of a new route forward. Connections to the cosmic whole are reestablished on entirely new foundations, anchored in previously unknown principles or archetypes. Individuals suddenly find themselves on a new level of development that they can barely comprehend. An epoch of great hope has arrived.
- PHASE THREE: It is time for new inspirations and plans to become reality in everyday practice. New cultures blossom. Individuals are involved in creative processes that reshape life, art, and religion, and creative exchange is fostered by newly emerging personal and social communication. Life teems with abundance and new courage.

- This cannot last forever, though. Occasional incidents and breakdowns indicate that the current stage of evolution has become outdated. Humankind is forced to come to grips with the first phase once again.

The Soul Layer of the Land

We owed our first insights into the relationship between the three countries of our pilgrimage and the threefold pattern of biblical migration to a "landscape constellation" inspired by Bert Hellinger's work with "family constellations." In geomancy, a landscape constellation is staged by constructing an imaginative model of a landscape in which individuals or small groups identify selected places. Assignment of roles is based on prior experience with the places in question. In addition, rituals are used to establish connections with the respective places on the energetic level. The result is the development of resonances that permit deeper insights into the inner world of individual places. Often insights into the landscape as a whole also rise to consciousness.

On April 13, 2001, after an exhausting day on the bus traveling east from Cairo, we spent the night near St. Catherine's Monastery at the foot of Mount Sinai. The next day, our travel group staged a landscape constellation in the geographic center of the Sinai Peninsula, not far from the Mount. We separated into small groups representing each of the special places we had already visited en route. (Of course we had not merely visited as tourists but had also attempted to perceive the different geomantic layers of these sites. After each visit, we had formed a circle and shared experiences, interpreting the holistic organism of the place together.) As the model of our threefold landscape came together, I was privileged to stand outside the group to observe the large-scale relationships. Once the small groups had tuned in to their places and established connections with each other, a strong energy field began to develop as the model gradually came to life. With my inner vision, I first saw a bright light flaring up at the point where the Nile forks to form its delta. This bright light spread out toward the east in the form of a semicircle. Over the Sinai Peninsula, this arc of light swung upright, forming half a dome, and then suddenly stopped. The dome's entire second half, which would have had to come from the west, from Israel, remained missing. I noted with interest that the missing half belonged to the area our group had not yet experienced at all. It made sense that the two halves should meet over Sinai, as suggested by the peninsula's location between the two countries.

These thoughts drew my attention to Sinai itself, and then something astonishing happened. In my mind's eye, I saw an inverted half sphere beginning to form underground. Like a great bowl of light, it stretched from the Nile to the Jordan. I was thrilled by the power and archetypal quality of this subterranean hemisphere. Deeply immersed in the three countries' subconscious, it represented the potential for them to come together again.

After tuning in to the bowl, I noticed that it was far from empty. In the Sinai area, it seemed to be filled with dynamic turbulence. I interpreted these swirling patterns as archetypal forces from the center of the Earth; together with the archetypes of earth-consciousness, they form the storehouse from which all life-forms on the Earth's surface draw nourishment and intelligence. In this context, it seemed that Sinai's role was to gather archetypal forces of life and consciousness underground and prepare them to manifest on the level of everyday life.

Our group had actually already decoded Sinai's hidden role halfway across the peninsula, en route to St. Catherine's Monastery. We had decided to stop at some inconsequential spot along the way to observe the desert we were driving through. We dispersed into the burned-out landscape, which was fully exposed to the sun's glare and showed almost no traces of vegetation. When we came together again and shared our individual experiences and observations, we noted a high degree of consistency. In spite of the barrenness of the landscape, we had all noticed that the prevailing mood was cheerful, pervaded with an invisible abundance of life. One woman even called it a "birthing mood," while I summed up my perceptions in the phrase "a nursery for elemental forces."

From my experiences in geomancy, I am familiar with places where the Earth's archetypal consciousness—Gaia or, if you will, the Earth Soul—is undergoing something like a "pregnant" phase. In these locations, the wild, untamed forces of the Earth's depths are adapting to the requirements of life on the surface. To put it differently, nature's young cells of consciousness are nourished and readied for life processes in the biosphere. Such landscapes (or at least all the examples I know of) are anything but lush—high alpine landscapes, moors, or desert-like places such as Sinai.

In reference to the human body, Sinai is the functional equivalent of the back. We usually give no thought to the system of forces occupying our back, which almost totally eludes our consciousness. In comparison to the lively creativity exercised by the front half of the body, the "landscape" of the back is as barren as a desert. Geomantic observation of this landscape confirms that a quiet dynamic prevails there, concentrating subconscious forces as yet unformed and unimpacted by everyday information. The human back develops into a storehouse of cosmic knowledge, a reservoir of archetypal forces from which the "I" draws the capacity to uphold the flow of life and the intelligence of the individual's essence. The back is a "holy space" where alchemical transformation occurs, allowing invisible worlds to manifest in etheric, conscious, and material forms. Our landscape constellation at the foot of Mount Sinai confirmed for us that the human body can indeed serve as an excellent model for revealing profound relationships in our landscapes. For example, likening the Sinai Peninsula to the invisible space of the human back is entirely congruent with the subterranean "storehouse" I perceived during the constellation.

At this point, let me tell you about the sight that met our eyes after we had crossed the border between Egypt and Israel, leaving Sinai's desert landscape behind us. As we arrived at the southernmost tip of Israel, we saw spread out before us the lush landscape of Elat, on the Red Sea coast, with its magnificent vegetation. Shortly before, we had been surrounded by Sinai's barren loneliness, and now we were suddenly overwhelmed with light and abundant life. Retaining the metaphor of the human body, we might say that in crossing Sinai, we had traveled along the back from the neck to the coccyx. Arriving in the water-rich landscape of Elat felt as if our route was now leading between the legs and through the genital area to the light at the front of the body.

After getting our bearings in this new landscape, we realized that we were standing at the base of a spatial axis that runs through Israel/Palestine from top to bottom, like a spine. This axis is clearly defined in the landscape by the Jordan rift valley, a deep indentation in the earth's crust. Its southern half is a dry streambed, but the upper portion, north of the Dead Sea, is enlivened by the Jordan River. The sources of the Jordan lie far to the north on the Syrian border, at the foot of Mount Hermon (a holy site in the local tradition). It's easy to imagine this site as corresponding to the human "crown chakra," which sits like a crown on the top of the head. The energetic spine of Israel/Palestine runs between the root-center "down below" on the Red Sea and Mount Hermon "up above" and is strung with a series of additional vital-energetic centers corresponding to the front chakras in the human being. En route, our group of pilgrims investigated the two that relate to the solar plexus and the larynx.

Most dramatic was the discovery of the country's solar plexus at Masada, an impressive mesa rising high above the plains around the Dead Sea. Masada is a key tourist attraction in Israel. Everyone traveling through the country insists on visiting the place where nine hundred Jews under siege by the Romans committed suicide almost two thousand years ago. For us, this history was reason enough to exclude Masada from our original itinerary, but as we approached we were unable to resist its call. A glance at the map of Israel confirms that Masada deserved our undivided attention. It is impossible to overlook the fact that the mesa lies exactly in the middle of the Jordan rift valley, like the navel in the human body. As such, Masada represents the country's geomantic center. It is Israel's *omphalos* or spiritual navel, the sunlike center from which Palestine's essential qualities radiate throughout the land.

Above and beyond its current, largely chaotic condition, Masada revealed itself to us as a holographic fragment of the country as a whole. The tabletop of the mountain has the shape of a mandorla. From its northern point to the middle, the element of water is at work, while the element of fire works from the south. The effects of these two elements meet in the middle, where the domelike element of air prevails. Similarly, Palestine itself is characterized by the water of the Jordan River north of the Red Sea and by the blazing heat of the barren riverbed to the south.

Continuing to follow Israel's "spine" northward, we come to the Sea of Galilee. If Elat on the Red Sea corresponds to the root chakra in humans and Masada on the Dead Sea to the solar plexus, then the Sea of Galilee corresponds to the larynx, the organ of speech. It is no coincidence that Jesus proclaimed his message from the Sea of Galilee two thousand years ago. This is a landscape of revelation.

When we observe the flow of energy along Israel's axis with this type of inner vision, we understand the enormous expansion of the larynx center in the Sea of Galilee. "Down below" at the Red Sea, a breath of air begins to form and then streams in a broad arc up to the Dead Sea. The Dead Sea sits in a deep depression (below sea level) that functions as a breathing hole, drawing the stream of energy down into the Earth. The breath's creative forces then flow underground in an arc to the Sea of Galilee. Directly above the Sea of Galilee, I perceived an etheric sphere that works like the human larynx. The interaction between the rising breath and the watery membrane of the lake's surface functions like a system of vocal cords, articulating the Word and breathing it out into the landscape through the etheric sphere.

Where is the heart-center of Israel's landscape temple, which must lie somewhere between the navel and the larynx? Where else but Jerusalem? Like the heart in the human body, Jerusalem lies to the left of the "spine" or axis that runs in an almost straight line between Elat and Mount Hermon. In landscapes, we often confront riddles that cannot be solved by linear thinking, and so it was this time. The route of our pilgrimage led from the Pyramids across Sinai to the Red Sea and then north to the Sea of Galilee. When we turned around and swung back south toward Jerusalem, I had the unmistakable impression that we had arrived in the center of a new space. I saw an almost unimaginable expanse centered on Jerusalem, a rounded energy field encompassing Asia Minor, the eastern end of the Mediterranean, most of Europe, and the northern part of Africa.

As a matter of fact, medieval maps of the world placed Jerusalem in the center, in the navel, with the then-known continents and countries grouped around it. Today we find these maps an amusing expression of either ignorance or religious zeal; we no longer appreciate the advantages of geographical maps that express the soul-dimension of space in the absence of information on the physical plane.

In my opinion Jerusalem, located in the center of this monumental space, serves as a focus for the force of attraction that holds the entire space together. Jerusalem's enormous power and heart-like quality are fed from the depths of the Pacific Ocean on the other side of the globe. We must imagine this connection as spiritual, not physical. In a sense, Jerusalem is the center of the world, drawing its strength from the infinite stillness of the ocean.

But let us not deceive ourselves. Jerusalem today is the exact opposite. Hotly contested for centuries, degraded by various religions into a fetish of their faith, and dominated by countless rulers in turn, Jerusalem has seen its original attributes largely suppressed. And yet, beneath the ashes, the intention of the Earth Soul is clear: to allow the rays of worldwide connection to shine forth again.

In the landscapes we are concerned with here, where would we find the head? In Sinai, we experienced the country's back and its archetypal forces. Then we traveled along the axis of the body, past the navel to the larynx, and then headed "down" to Jerusalem in a dramatic reversal of direction. Had we totally bypassed the head?

By no means. But to find the head, we must remember that multidimensional space is never flat. It is always curved in a certain way. Wouldn't it be ideal if the end of our pilgrimage from Egypt via Sinai to Israel linked up with the beginning again? This possibility is exactly what was whispered to me as I prepared for the closing meditation of our trip on April 23, 2001.

In this meditation, I wanted to lead the group along the route of our journey again, experiencing it literally in our own bodies. While preparing for the meditation, I noticed some internal uncertainty as to where to begin. Our journey had begun at the Pyramids of Giza, as if at the back of the head, and then proceeded down the backbone, but whether the plateau of Giza actually corresponded to the head remained an unanswered question.

I asked my inner master to show me which part of my body resonated with the starting point of our journey. I had scarcely formulated the question when I was led abruptly to the back of my head, where I saw to my astonishment the Sphinx and the Pyramids of Cheops, Chefren, and Mycerinus, as if they had been standing there forever. When I looked around me, it was like looking out from the pyramid complex onto the entire universe, complete with stars and planets and the spiritual worlds associated with them. I felt as if my neck was supporting a skull of crystal.

This surprising role of the Giza plateau had already been suggested to me during preparations for the pilgrimage, but I had not understood because I lacked experience with the actual landscape. At that time, I was using geographical maps in my attempts to establish contact with the three countries we planned to visit. As I did so, my interest in the soul level of these three countries was selectively awakened. My perceptions at that time revealed the following patterns:

- EGYPT (in this case, North Egypt, centered on the Giza pyramid complex) appeared to me as the virginal figure of a black Goddess. A surprising sensation of shock overcame me in the moment of perception, and the black color of the virgin's skin shone with such force that it seemed to point to a hidden mystery. But as I mentioned before, the plateau's mysterious role was revealed to me only at the end of our trip, after I had experienced it in the center of my head. Along with a very few other places of this sort, the holon or holistic network of the three Pyramids plus the Sphinx anchors the wisdom and love of the entire universe to the Earth.
- SINAI appeared to my mind's eye as a red-tinted energy field. In the words we usually use to distinguish various aspects of the cosmic soul or Goddess, red symbolizes the forces of creation. Only after experiencing the Sinai Peninsula as a storehouse of archetypal forces was I able to interpret this red color correctly in relationship to the landscape. It stands for the fiery mass of archetypal, as yet undifferentiated life forces that fill Sinai's subterranean reservoir.
- ISRAEL/PALESTINE, associated as it is with conflict, could well have been represented by the color black, but to my surprise, I perceived the soul of the country as a crystalline, totally unclouded white! I was inspired by the beauty and strength that radiated from the Goddess of the country. As we have learned in the meantime, Israel/Palestine represents the sun-filled, embodied aspect of life, so the clarity of its presence is easy to interpret. The white radiance was so bright that its higher-level message was impossible to ignore: Palestine has something vitally important to tell us human beings!

I should also mention that in my inner perception, these three countries were cloaked in a cloud of sorrow, and I heard a female voice singing an endless dirge. I experienced a dramatic discrepancy between the soul-identity of the three countries and the reality of their current situation. The dirge pointed to the fundamental perversion that had ruthlessly estranged the countries of the Near East from their soul-spiritual essence.

The night after asking for help in preparing for the task that awaited us in the Near East, I also had a dream suggestive of the fundamental problem of these three countries on the soul level. I saw a flat, lifeless wall that was infinitely high, long, and broad. It covered everything. From the center of the wall hung a limp but still living penis, apparently the genital organ of an old man. Against the backdrop of the lifeless wall, the warmth of his blood screamed of tragedy.

This dream was so perplexing and ambiguous, I didn't dare to tell my traveling companions about it. Only through our experiences en route from Cairo to Jerusalem did I become aware of how dominant male-organized, patriarchal cultures and religions are in the Near East and how heavily they still influence all levels of existence. I do not mean to say that this patriarchal orientation served no purpose in the past, but it is a shock to realize the extent to which male values have led to both visible and invisible (but all the more brutal) systemic violence. The machinery of violence holds up the wall of my dream and completely masks the true multidimensional being of the local landscape, not to mention human wholeness, both of which have been abandoned to almost total alienation.

Landscape and Pilgrimage Merge

The discrepancy between the beauty and power of these three countries on the soul level and the entrenched patriarchy of daily life again raises the question of transformation. The birthing pangs of the Goddess of the land, which accompanied my perception, led me to understand that this shocking discrepancy could be resolved only through fundamental transformation.

- THE FIRST STAGE OF THE JOURNEY centers on the Giza plateau. Together with its Pyramids and Sphinx, the plateau radiates inspiration that allows us to glimpse the wholeness of our being. If there were no such places on Earth, we would lose all memory of our inmost being and of the meaning of life independent of space and time. This memory serves as a—possibly unconscious—challenge to free ourselves from mental and emotional entanglements. Without such opportunities to experience our wholeness, transformation could never occur. No vision would be profound enough to set transformation in motion. We would remain enslaved to our alienation for all eternity. There is no other way to express it: The archetypal journey from the Pyramids across Sinai to Jerusalem symbolizes the inner path leading to actualization of the integrated human being. This route, however, cannot be followed by individuals who are not ready to subject themselves to fundamental transformation.

- THE SECOND STAGE OF THE PATH OF TRANSFORMATION demands a certain separation from life's superficial rhythm. This stage is symbolized by the lengthy period of time the Israelites spent in the Sinai Desert before being ready to enter the Promised Land. In the loneliness of the desert, the individual is confronted with the need to transform the past and its oppressive patterns. On the other hand, as described in a previous chapter, Sinai also stands for the subterranean storehouse of forces needed to build up new connections and the foundations of a new culture. In the process of personal transformation, the second stage manifests as critical observation of one's own thoughts and actions. To disconnect from what is old and lifeless, each of us must decide again what is true for us and what is not.
- THE THIRD STAGE embodies all the qualities that make up the integrated human being. The "eternal human"—that is, the aspect of ourselves that we normally equate with life after death—"marries" the bodily human being. The individual becomes free to take part in the uninterrupted creative dance of the earthly cosmos. This is the phase of mature human civilization, a culture of peace that invites not only humankind but all living and spiritual beings to join it. From the landscape perspective, we recognized this third stage, the stage of embodying the divine, in Israel/Palestine. *The acutely critical current situation in the Holy Land presents humankind with tasks that must be accomplished if our embodiment on Earth is to develop into a blessing for all beings and spheres of the universe.*

To help us experience as well as understand the meaning of journeying from the Pyramids across Sinai to Jerusalem, let me present this route in the form of a meditation:

Meditation

- Enter your inner stillness and spend some time in peace.
- Focus your feeling and consciousness in the back of your head and find its center. From this location, send a ray of light out through your third eye and anchor it in a distant point in the space in front of you. (Corresponds to the landscape of the Giza plateau.)
- Next, begin to construct a bridge of light behind you, running along your spine in the space behind your back. This bridge is not simply a straight line; it is branched on both sides like the antlers of a stag, and the branches are anchored in your back. (Corresponds to the Sinai Peninsula.)
- At the far end of the bridge, which rests on your sacrum, there is a gate. Go through it. You will find yourself in the rounded space of your abdomen. Here, anchor yourself deeply in the earth. (Corresponds to Elat on the Red Sea coast.)
- From the center of your abdomen, rise vertically until you reach the navel point above the solar plexus. Visualize countless rays of sunlight emerging from your solar plexus in all directions and anchoring you in your surroundings. (Corresponds to the Masada plateau above the Dead Sea.)
- Continue your vertical ascent past your heart to your larynx. Around your larynx, a crystal sphere forms. It contains the message of your innermost being. (Corresponds to the Sea of Galilee.)
- Take the crystal sphere in your hands, carry it down through the space in front of you, and place it in your heart. At this moment, your heart begins to radiate love-energy and the message of your essential being. (Jerusalem)
- How does it feel to stand in the middle of the cosmos, radiating love?

A Series of Heart-Centers

In reflecting on the route of our pilgrimage thus far, we have been moving about primarily on the landscape's soul-spiritual level. This is the layer or dimension of space that is closest to my heart, so I felt responsible for decoding it during the trip. Geomancy usually uses the term "landscape temple" to describe a country's soul layer. In this case, "temple" refers not to a structure but to an invisible, subtle, and all-pervading layer in space that corresponds qualitatively to the attributes of the human soul. This subtle membrane is anchored in specific locations in each landscape and becomes perceptible through the constellation of the anchor points and their various energetic functions. In this sense, we might refer to the composition of the landscapes of North Egypt, Sinai, and Israel/Palestine as a landscape temple of the Near East, with each country also being pervaded by a landscape temple of its own.

So as not to neglect other layers of space, my daughter Ana Pogačnik, who co-led the trip with me, focused on the landscape's vital layer, the bioenergetic web that pervades places and landscapes and imbues them with life-energy. This vital-energetic web consists of energy-centers, lines, and fields. Thanks to messages Ana received directly from the angelic world, we were initiated into the mysteries of the vital-energetic dimension of the places we visited. Most impressive was the series of heart-centers in North Egypt, Sinai, and Jerusalem, which Ana pointed out to us along our route.

Like the heart chakra in the human being, the Earth's heart-centers work on several different levels. On the vital level, the heart-center of a landscape is responsible for renewing its life forces. The depleted forces from Earth's surface are inhaled by the regional heart-center, imbued with fresh life-information, and then given back to the landscape.

On the soul level, heart-centers serve as ambassadors of the love-energy that Sister Earth bestows incessantly on all the beings that live on her. The love radiating from the center of our loving, conscious planet invites all of us to the dance of love that imparts a paradisiacal quality to life on Earth (if we let it). This is no mere memory of Paradise Lost or a past Golden Age described by the traditions and scriptures of various cultures. Rather, it is a real opportunity to enjoy the paradisiacal quality of life in us and around us, here and now. This opportunity is maintained without interruption by the Earth's heart-system, but to make it a reality in our everyday personal and social life, we as individuals would first have to get to know the depths of our own heart-centers and the energy that radiates from them and then bring this energy to expression.

We must be careful, however, not to imagine planet Earth's heart system in overly anthropomorphic terms. Gaia does not pour her forces of life and love out through a single "Earth heart chakra." The Earth's heart is organized in such a way that every little bit of the globe's surface, as well as entire countries and continents, can share her blessings of love and renewal. Individual heart-centers throughout the world pulsate and resonate with each other, forming a global network that is the Earth's actual heart system. This heart-network incorporates not only the countless tiny heart-centers of individual places but also the huge heart chakras of larger territories such as North Egypt, Sinai, and Jerusalem.

- THE HEART-CENTER OF NORTH EGYPT was originally located on the Giza plateau, and in fact that is where it still pulsates today. Its site, however, was reshaped by the ancient Egyptians into the giant sculpture of the Sphinx, carved out of the rock of the plateau. Today North Egypt's heart-center is located in the chest of the mysterious Sphinx. I see it pulsing there like a magnificent ruby.
- THE SINAI HEART-CENTER is the site of the famous St. Catherine's Monastery. This Orthodox compound has survived as a monastery since the founding years of Christianity. Muslim conquerors spared it during their campaigns because of its association with Moses, who is held in high regard in the Koran. The monastery and the heart-center are located at the foot of Mount Sinai, where Moses received the Ten Commandments from God's own hand, according to biblical accounts.
- THE HEART-CENTER OF JERUSALEM is centered in the depths of the hill of Golgotha, where Jesus was crucified together with the two thieves. The foot of the rocky slope is now occupied by the gigantic Dome of the Rock. In its crypt, which is as close as one can get to the heart-center today, I perceived the heart-center in the form of two radiant bands of light, one vertical (reaching from heaven to Earth) and one horizontal. These bands were rotating around each other. The horizontal band refers to the spectrum of beings and forces that make up the web of life.

These three super-regional heart-centers have the power to determine the quality of space in the Near East. Love is meant to be a fundamental quality pervading the landscapes and cities of this territory, but unfortunately it is suppressed at its source. Although hordes of thirsting tourists are drawn to the Pyramids and the Sphinx, their guides take them right past the source of love itself, directing their interest away from the true treasure of the place. They are told only about the mysterious past, the Egyptian cult of the dead, and the site's astronomical connections. Nothing else. This misdirection of attention is one of the factors blocking the energy of this site.

At Jerusalem's heart-center, I perceived a different problem. Because the emotional layer of a place plays a crucial part in how easily it is permeated by heart pulsations, I tuned in to this layer. It was anything but pretty! In various locations within the city, I saw holes with all sorts of refuse, ruins, and rigid thought forms spilling out of them and darkening the sky. How can the heart-center possibly pulse freely with the quality of love in a place that is so polluted on the feeling level?

The Planet's Grounding Center

Surely the most impressive energy-center that Ana showed us en route was the planetary grounding center. To refer again to the chakras of the human body, this is the equivalent of the root chakra, located on the coccyx, which grounds human energy systems in the earth.

Since humans are highly dynamic beings, moving here, there and everywhere, it only makes sense that they need grounding. But why does the static, immobile Earth itself need grounding? The Earth itself is very well grounded, but over the course of millions of years its surface space has become richly subdivided. This space consists of energy fields, emotional "clouds," layers of consciousness, subtle membranes, and diverse biotopes. Unimaginable confusion would result if all these surface phenomena were not anchored—"grounded"—in the Earth's center.

Just as gravitation ensures grounding on the physical plane, so too there are vital-energetic earth centers that maintain the inherent structure of the etheric extension of space. This function became especially important after we humans created a mentally advanced civilization that always tends to "take off" and build castles in the air, placing extreme demands on the grounding centers.

Again, the grounding centers include both small ones that ground individual places and gigantic ones that serve the planet as a whole. One of the latter is found in the area of the Dead Sea. The Dead Sea's surface four hundred meters below sea level, and the sea itself is another four hundred meters deep. This is the deepest point on the Earth's surface, an ideal spot for grounding Earth's branching energy systems.

On the planetary scale, the Earth's grounding system consists of five energy-centers, one of which—according to one of the messages Ana received from the angelic world—is to be found at the Dead Sea. These centers emerge at various points on the planet and are rooted in its core.

As our group attempted to sense the quality of the Earth's grounding center, an image appeared to me. I saw a tightly closed bud with its stem extending deep into the ground, but no roots were evident. Instead, I had the feeling that the flower on top of that tall stem was unstable and might fall over at any moment. As my inner vision became more focused, I was able to take a closer look. What was the matter with the roots? But now, at the base of the stem, I saw a corona of very delicate young roots developing. We interpreted this as a favorable sign of a self-healing process in progress in the Earth's root chakra.

A Hodgepodge of Religions in the Land's Consciousness Layer

So far, we have considered our pilgrimage from the Pyramids across Sinai to Jerusalem on two levels. We turned first to the soul-spiritual layer of the land and wandered through its landscape temple. Seeking correspondences with the human body, we explored the head and back of the countryside as well as its sunlit front. Then we turned our attention to the vital-energetic layer of the three countries. We saw some of the most important energy-centers of North Egypt, Sinai, and Israel/Palestine. To continue with the comparison to the human body, we might equate the energy-layer of a landscape to the legs. Just as the legs make it possible for the body to move about, so too the vital systems of a landscape serve to bring streams of life into motion.

In our attempts to understand the landscape as a whole, we are still missing the correspondence to the second set of extremities, our hands. Hands can be seen as a spatial extension of the larynx chakra in that hands transform the creative imagination that comes about in the larynx into action. In comparison to the creative processes taking place in a landscape, we might identify the hands' function with the consciousness layer of space. In the context of the natural world, "consciousness" means the elemental beings and nature spirits that initiate and guide life processes. They represent the Earth's consciousness, which works through the landscape. They are like the Earth's active, creative hands.

But because landscapes are also populated by human beings, a second aspect of consciousness becomes active in space. This is the consciousness of local cultures. Patterns and flows of thought created by the thinking, feeling, and willing of the local people pervade the landscape and leave decisive imprints on its qualitative aspect. Such imprints were especially apparent to our group. At every turn, we encountered important artistic and cultural monuments from different epochs, each with its own story to tell. The vibrations of these stories spread out over the landscape in the form of mental and emotional fields. In the territory between the Pyramids and Jerusalem, fields with religious imprints are especially evident.

With regard to the consciousness layer of the land, we had decided even before setting out on the trip to concentrate primarily on religious energy fields. We did not ignore the elemental beings and nature spirits, however, but included them in our geomantic investigations of individual places. But why did we want to pay particular attention to the religious fields?

It is impossible to overlook the decisive impulses for human religious life that emerged in the Near East and in Israel/Palestine in particular. If we look only at those impulses that have withstood the test of millennia and still shape humankind today, we must think first and foremost of the covenant the Jews entered into with their God in the Sinai desert. In the context of this covenant, the manifestation of the Christ on Earth became possible. Jerusalem is also one of the three most important holy cities of Islam because Mohammed's ascent into heaven occurred there.

To sense the quality of these diverse religious fields, our group visited the holy places of Judaism, Christianity, and Islam as we traveled from Egypt across Sinai and on to Jerusalem. In synagogues, mosques, and churches, we opened ourselves repeatedly to subtle perceptions and then shared our experiences. Then we decided in common whether or not the group had anything to contribute toward healing the place in question.

Let me make it clear that our group was not at all interested in *historical* accounts of the three religions and their sacred sites but only in their role in humankind's *spiritual* evolution. We were inspired by one possible interpretation of the term "religion," which is derived from the Latin root *religio*. Thus "religion" means something like "reconnection." In the original sense of the word, it did not mean an organized group of believers in a specific faith. Rather, it referred to the revelation and communication of specific spiritual tools that help individuals reconnect with their true beings.

The concept of reconnection assumes that modern individuals exist only as partial human beings, cut off from their multidimensional wholeness. As a consequence of a process that has been going on for several millennia, we have become increasingly entrenched in the loneliness of our keen intellect and its materialistic ideas. During the Iron Age, human beings lost the connection to those aspects of their wholeness that proved they were part of both the earthly natural world as a whole and the eternal, spiritual world.

"To reconnect" in this sense means to follow a path that makes it possible for us to develop and solidify living connections to the separated or suppressed dimensions of our own being and to make these connections a reality in our everyday life. But because we are essentially different as individuals and belong to different traditions, a variety of "religions"—i.e., collections of spiritual tools—developed to do justice to our differing needs with regard to reconnection.

If different world religions, or even local religious movements, developed out of the desire for reconnection, this means that they were not originally present. Originally, human beings were part of the cosmic and earthly whole. When we were first created by the forces of nature and born out of the primal space of eternity, we needed no religion. We began to need tools for reconnecting ourselves only later, when social norms and educational practices had begun to alienate us from our own wonderful wholeness. Consequently, we will no longer need the support of religion once we have learned to protect our children from this process of alienation and to permanently anchor our own wholeness in our hearts and manifest it freely in our lives.

It stands to reason, therefore, that the three religions of Judaism, Christianity, and Islam were originally created to support our evolution toward true humanity. But when we consider these three religious edifices with all their institutions, precepts, and moral restraints, it is difficult to avoid the conclusion that they have long since become alienated from their original purpose in the course of their development in their respective cultures and societies.

In this sense, religions should "reconnect" with their original purpose, too. As we visited the holy places of Christianity, Judaism, and Islam in our travels from Cairo across Sinai to Jerusalem, our group searched for opportunities to link these religions to their original task. We firmly believe that the prerequisites for lasting peace in the Near East will be created when these three religions reconnect with the divine intention that brought them into being.

Experiencing the Coptic Energy Field

In Cairo's Old Town, the holy sites of Coptic Christianity reminded us of the original intention that led to the founding of religions. In the Coptic churches and monasteries our group visited, I perceived a heavenly potency in the quality of the light that is not often found in Christian sanctuaries. Jill Kamil's book on Coptic Egypt, which I purchased at the gates of one of the monasteries, brought clarification. Until then, I had associated Coptic

Christianity with Ethiopia, but Ms. Kamil draws a clear line from the Pharaonic Empire to the Hellenistic period in Egypt to the founding of the autonomous Coptic Church, which still exists today. She makes it clear that "Coptic" essentially means "Egyptian."

An experience in the "Hanging Church" of the Virgin Mary was especially meaningful to me. Although Mass was being celebrated, and the church was filled with believers, we were able to find a space to sit and conduct our "inner child" exercise. In this exercise, you imagine holding yourself as a small child in your arms and observing the surrounding space through the child's eyes. In this instance, the "inner child" stands for the eternal soul in each of us, which knows no spatial and temporal constraints and is free of the preconceived ideas and desires of the personality of the outer Self.

I attempted this exercise several times, and each time the inner child on my lap turned around and looked me in the eye. At first I thought it wanted to tell me something I was not yet open to receiving. I understood its true message only when my attention was drawn to the enclosed space created by the child's gesture. Its feet merged with my genitals and its head with my throat. Its little body arched outward, and the hollow space between our hearts began to shine. The shining grew ever stronger until it extended far into our surroundings.

This gesture reminded me of another inner perception I had had the day before as we stood in front of the statues of the Pharaoh Ikhnaton in Cairo's Egyptian Museum. The perspectives of earthly and cosmic creative energies were so closely linked in the statue that the synthesis of these two opposites began to shine.

On April 10, 2001, the day before we began our pilgrimage, I insisted on viewing the relics of the Amarna culture in the Egyptian Museum. Intuition told me that the revelation of human wholeness in the Near East had been preceded by a relatively short but important phase in Egypt, initiated by the Pharaoh Ikhnaton, who declared the sun-god Aton to be the only true god. For a short span of a few decades, a monotheistic religion prevailed in Egypt, in stark contrast to the ancient polytheistic belief system. This monotheistic period was associated with the cultural developments now known as the culture of Tell el Amarna.

Aton-worship is generally seen as an early form of belief in God the Father, but my experience in the Egyptian Museum convinced me that it was actually an early manifestation of the cosmic energy that later, through Coptic Christianity, became known as Christ-consciousness. When I found the appropriate room in the museum, I was surprised to discover a union of opposites in that all of the larger-than-life statues of the Pharaoh had distinctly female hips but male facial traits. Focusing my inner vision on the sculptures confirmed that this was no mere coincidence but a message, which I then perceived in a sequence of inner pictures.

I first saw a powerful stream of earthly energy rising through the Pharaoh's legs and pouring into the statue's broad hips. A huge explosion of light occurred when this energy stream reached the navel. But what triggered it? As I pursued this question, I perceived that an opposing process was also at work. A bundle of cosmic energy was flowing downward through the Pharaoh's head. It looked like a spool of cosmic energy unwinding high above his head. In the area around the navel, these two force-streams met, giving birth to light.

I experienced a similar synthesis of upper and lower in the Coptic church when my inner child—that is, the eternal in me—merged with the creative organs of the embodied, earthly human being. Heaven and Earth entered into an astonishing synthesis symbolized by the light-filled space that developed between me and the child.

When we experience this synthesis, we feel simultaneously connected to the earthly and cosmic extensions of our own being, but the threads that bind the two together again run inward, not outward. We are not simply reconnecting with the divine in the universe or in the Earth's center, as was the case in ancient Egyptian culture of the pre-Amarna periods. Instead, we experience the merging of the earthly and spiritual extensions of our own being and recognize the creative potential concealed within. The creative dance of life turns outward only after this inner "core fusion" is complete.

Thanks to the inspiration of the Pharaoh Ikhnaton, the possibility of a creative synthesis of heaven and earth *within the human being* lit up for the first time, although it was extinguished with comet-like rapidity. The energy field of human consciousness was not yet mature enough to absorb this revolutionary innovation.

My experience with my inner child in the Coptic church, however, provided a perspective on the synthesis between heaven and earth that I had not noticed in the statues of Ikhnaton. When the child turned around to face me, we looked each other in the eyes. I felt this as an individual call for each human being to set out on a personal path to self-knowledge. Only when the synthesis of time and eternity has become an inner reality for each of us, in our own individual ways, will it also become a lasting source of peace in the society of which we all are part.

It is significant that the Coptic and Orthodox churches parted company over the question of the relationship between time and eternity in 451 A.D., when the split was finalized at the Council of Chalcedon. The Egyptians, who refused to accept the dogma that two separate natures—human/earthly and spiritual/divine—were united in the Christ, were then called Monophysites, which means nothing more than that they believed in the Christ as a unitary presence that is of divine nature. Since that time, the Coptic Church has been independent, with its own doctrine, style of art, and ecclesiastical hierarchy.

Experiencing the Jewish Energy Field

Our tour group first came into contact with the Jewish religion's energy field in the synagogue of Old Cairo, which dates from the twelfth century A.D. It was built on the site where the Church of the Archangel Michael once stood. As I tuned in to the energy field of the place, the first thing I saw was two huge cylinders of white light, like two columns. They reminded me of the double scroll of the Jewish Torah. Between the two columns there was room enough to allow a broad ray of divine blessing to stream down to Earth. But almost instantly the two columns began to move closer together and the space between them narrowed, leaving ever less space for the divine ray to get through, until it was extinguished completely. Then the space was filled with the vibrations of a profound sadness. In the midst of the sadness, I perceived a field of hope and expectation, but it seemed threatened.

Other members of our group mentioned the Star of David, and in fact the two columns of light in my vision can be equated with the two triangles of the Star of David, which represent the perfect connection between heaven and Earth that allows the divine to be revealed. The fact that the two columns of light moved closer together, extinguishing the radiance of the divine, could easily be interpreted in a negative sense, as the Twilight of the Gods, but I heard an inner call to see it as something positive. In other words, the revelation of God as it shone out in the past—think of Moses' illumination on Mount Sinai—evolves over time, as symbolized by the movement of the columns. Beginning with the moment of divine revelation, evolution undergoes different stages until its message is acknowledged in the inner world of every individual participating in the energy field of the religion in question.

The force of revelation only seems to disappear. Quite understandably, it chooses to disappear as an external force in order to manifest directly and practically in the life of each individual until it is again present in all its fullness. The problem for us is that it is much easier to attribute the power of the divine to a distant epoch of revelation than to admit it into our personal present. Out of fear, we always attempt to maintain an objective distance from the divine, because when divine energy gains admission to our inner world, it unleashes incredibly turbulent transformations. We shy away from this possibility.

As I see it, within the field of the Jewish religion, this fear has led to tension that is now calling for release. On the one hand, divine revelation is praised and worshiped but too often relegated to the past; a fateful sense of separation from it produces the profound sorrow that accompanied my vision. On the other hand, the coming of the Messiah, who will bring a divine quality to life on Earth for all times to come, is expected in the future. This is why I also perceived an energy field of hope.

A religious consciousness that dwells constantly on the past and projects all its expectations into the future creates two complementary dead ends that allow us to escape from the divine presence in the here and now. We remain caught in this division, which evokes only an illusion of connectedness instead of true reconnection with the whole. To put it differently, by satisfying religious precepts, we live in the illusion of having found our own wholeness. Incidentally, this applies not only to Judaism but also to the contemporary religious practices of Islam and Christianity.

I was moved to make this statement by a second vision, which I experienced on a return visit to the synagogue. The figure of one of the ancestors of the Jewish people, presumably one of the biblical Prophets, appeared out of primal space, with an imploring look in his eyes. When I asked what he wanted of me, a simple affirmation resounded: "No separation." I sensed how painful it must be for the spirit of a religion to remain chained in the prison of the past—or of the future.

Experiencing the Islamic Energy Field

Immediately after visiting the synagogue of Old Cairo, we became aware of the inherent problematic of the Islamic path to reconnection when our group visited the Mosque of Al-Ghuri. In every single room, the guide showed us the symbolic door that is always aligned with Mecca.

From the geomantic perspective, I have always been fascinated by the phenomenon of hundreds of millions of believers throughout the world homing in on one and the same point on the Earth's surface on a daily basis—the point marked by the sacred stone, the black meteorite of the Kaaba in Mecca. No other religion understands how to cultivate its center as well as Islam, which is organized as a sphere-like network around this sacrosanct navel stone or *omphalos*. In terms of the human body, this is the energy of the center, which is focused in the solar plexus. We can imagine how powerful this centering energy becomes when it is repeatedly evoked by multitudes of people worldwide at rhythmical intervals.

I had already had many opportunities to experience the power of this collective centering in the mosques of Sarajevo. Within a so strongly centralized entity, one's particular location, be it in Africa, Asia, or the Balkans, is more or less irrelevant. The identity of the place is unimportant, since we are all drawn to the same point—the "world navel," the Black Stone of the Kaaba. Concentrating on this point in common is intended to make it relatively easy to sense the qualities of divine omnipotence, clarity of intention, and even psychological security and to feel embedded in them. Nonetheless, I wonder what happens to the individual aspect of the path to reconnection. Doesn't this distinctly collective way of connecting to the center endanger the diversity of individual paths to wholeness and thus also our tolerance toward others?

On April 10, 2001, as I stood in the Mosque of Al-Ghuri, the eyes of my soul were opened to perceive again the central energy field of the Muslim world. I was suddenly struck with the frightening premonition that this idyllic image of collective connection to the omnipotent divine was subject to an illusion of some sort. Of course I wanted to check this feeling out. At that moment, the world-wide, center-oriented Islamic energy field began to move wildly. In addition to feeling great astonishment, I also sensed a great threat. Presumably this latter sensation was responsible for the sudden appearance of a djinn-like figure. I was confronted by one of the mighty guardians of Islamic culture, who issued a graphic ban on further research. I complied.

I would have forgotten this incident, but a few months later the attacks of September 11, 2001 occurred, implemented in cold blood by devout elements of Islam's central energy field. I spent three days in a state of spiritual shock. On the fourth day, I abruptly decided to write a book entitled *The Koran for Christians*. In view of the concrete threat of escalating violence overshadowing connections between the Islamic and Christian worlds, my inspiration at that time was to promote peaceful exchanges between these two religious consciousness fields. I thought the western world needed to learn from Islamic teachings the importance of focusing on a common universal center. Conversely, I thought it would be a blessing for members of the Islamic community to receive the West's gifts of individuation and inner independence. Through mutual fructification and by receiving each other's gifts, the two world religions would be able to enter into peaceful dialogue in a single, higher-ranking energy field that encompassed them both.

My thought was not that the Christian world should develop a centralized energy field like Islam's. Not at all! Christianity would continue to hold individuals responsible for their own lives and to cultivate its religion of personal love and freedom. The Christian world would still be composed of countless free-floating entities—an ideal structure, although it is constantly threatened by the Church's hierarchical and centralizing tendencies.

My thought was rather to overcome a specific obstacle. As a consequence of its inherent impulses for individuation and freedom, the Christian world too often succumbs to an egocentric position that allows its believers to exploit their surroundings and their contemporaries. Adopting the wisdom of centering in the Islamic sense would allow individuals to learn to tune in repeatedly to the divine core of the universe, thus overcoming the danger of egocentricity. In exchange, it would be beneficial for the members of the Islamic energy field to learn to disconnect themselves gradually from their shared center and find paths to their *personal* centers. Since divinity pulses at the core of each human being, the quality of togetherness would not be lost. In this sense, Islam and Christianity can certainly be understood as two complementary religions with the inherent capacity to correct and complement each other.

But my enthusiasm about the possibility of these two world religions mutually enriching each other was called into question by a dream that came to me soon after I had decided on the *Koran for Christians* project. In the dream, I saw our group in a bus, just as we had actually traveled from the Pyramids to Jerusalem. We were driving along the top of a tableland. It ended in a sharp point far in the distance, crowned with a glorious temple. I sensed very clearly that the divinity dwelt in the temple and that we absolutely had to go there. The monumental plateau, ending in a single point with a single temple, can be interpreted as the religious energy field dedicated to the divine in the monotheistic sense. Our group's bus trip toward the temple stands for the human longing for reconnection.

Suddenly an inner voice spoke to me, advising me against continuing in this direction. I was outraged. After all, our hearts' desire was to draw closer to the divine. But the voice said, "If you go there, you will be disappointed, and the way back is very long." In lieu of explanation, I was shown an enormous perpendicular notch carved into the plateau. Obviously the work of human hands, it threatened to split the unified plateau into two halves. Then I noticed for the first time that the plateau was deserted and empty. The notch, however, showed signs of daily activity. People had built their houses there wherever they pleased, each with a fence around it. Although the area seemed to be extremely densely populated, I repeatedly encountered abandoned spaces as I searched for someone who could explain the meaning of this parasitic world.

The dream's message was unmistakable. In my enthusiasm, I had confused the everyday reality of a world religion that had been involved for centuries in conquering countries and continents with the idealized conception of a religious field of consciousness. According to my dream, the original divine inspiration now serves as the foundation for the edifice of a world religion that to a large extent is pursuing the goal of self-preservation. Both Christianity and Islam are suffering under this shadow aspect.

Experiencing the Christian Energy Field

Our tour group experienced the shadow aspect of the Christian religion after reaching the Sea of Galilee. According to Gospel accounts, this is where Jesus was most active. We visited one common destination of pilgrims in the Holy Land that exemplified the fundamental alienation to which Christian reconnection has succumbed. The Sermon on the Mount is said to have taken place at a particular spot on the slope above the Sea of Galilee. There Jesus Christ proclaimed the words that became the foundation of the Christian religion. Not far from a rustling grove of ancient fig trees stands a modern basilica, a must-see stop on any "Bible tour" of the Holy land.

My experiences in this place were very depressing. In its present condition, the space could not possibly live up to the religious expectations imposed on it. I sensed a congestion of forces emanating from countless pilgrims consciously or unconsciously hoping to be touched by the Christ here in this place. But of course these expectations, contrasting starkly with the teachings of Jesus Christ, remained unfulfilled. If in fact God became human to teach us that the truth is found nowhere but in ourselves, it is very strange to see people seeking the truth by retracing his steps. In this context, let me quote a saying of the Christ from the Coptic Gospel according to Thomas: "He who knows the universe but fails to know himself fails to know the whole" (Saying 67). Other participants in our group also expressed their disappointment in this place. One of them formulated it like this: It is impossible to expect the spirit of God, who is present in every moment, to linger in memories of events that happened two thousand years ago.

After sharing our impressions, we walked down barely discernible trails to the lake. As I followed a path lined with golden blades of grass, I was suddenly electrified by a familiar feeling. My intuition immediately associated it with the quality I had experienced years ago during energy-work with the texts of the Gospels and interpreted as a sign of the presence of the Christ. This special feeling awakened my sensitivity, and I began to investigate the energy line that was perceptible along the path.

Subtle energy lines of this sort develop along regularly traveled pathways. When the energy fields of humans or animals constantly rub up against the energy field of the surrounding landscape, the result is a magnetic trace that can store living information. Tuning in to the path's energy line again, I could no longer shut out the fact that a memory of the Christ's presence is indeed engraved on the Palestinian landscape in certain places, where it still pulsates as a source of living energy and love and can be perceived as such. Assuming, of course, that it isn't blocked by false expectations, as was the case in the above-mentioned basilica.

- The Christ represents a cosmic principle that calls upon human beings to recognize divine forces and qualities in themselves, to cultivate these qualities individually and to make them a reality in their lives. It follows that the presence of the divine is to be found nowhere other than within us. Hence, we can find it wherever we happen to be at the moment, not just in Israel/Palestine. We do not need to travel to Judea in order to make progress toward becoming truly human. Eventually, our experiences with the Christ's presence in Israel/Palestine condensed into a multi-layered pattern:
- The Christ can also be understood as an aspect of the divine that decided to incarnate on Earth to show human beings the way to a new level of evolution. In geomantic terms, incarnation means not only manifesting in a human body but also becoming grounded or rooted in a specific place, i.e., the landscape surrounding the embodiment in question. In this sense, Israel/Palestine inherits a unique gift that all human beings can share if they are prepared to become involved in the landscape's deeper dimensions and to accept the personal transformation that results.
- Lastly, in certain places, it is possible to sense a living memory of the historical presence of the Christ and to trace the paths he took through Israel/Palestine, which were imprinted on the memory of the landscape. In these places, the stored information can be called up at any time as an inspirational experience, whenever we need it in our search for personal reconnection. We need to be careful, however, to seek out places that have not been chaotically impacted by later human activity.

Unfortunately, the religious zeal and curiosity of Christian pilgrims are among the most damaging disruptive factors.

Cooperation or Conflict?

Immersing ourselves in the spiritual atmosphere of places that Jews, Christians, and Muslims hold sacred allowed our group to gain insight into the deeper interrelationships among the three world religions. All three were founded in the Near East, although at different times. Most of the Bible is said to have been written in the ninth century B.C., thus laying the cornerstone for the Jewish religion. The Christ's three years of public activity at the beginning of the Common Era were followed by the development of the Christian Church. Between 610 and 632 A.D., Mohammed wrote down the Koran as dictated to him by the archangel Gabriel and brought Islam into being on the basis of this revelation.

The logical question is, since these three religions all relate to the same sources—i.e., holy places—in the landscape and appeared at rhythmical intervals, did they arise from a common nucleus? A few commonalities are generally known. For example, statements in Gospel accounts of the life and work of Jesus Christ are supported by quotations from Jewish scripture. This is why the Old Testament is included in the Christian Bible. In 662, Mohammed was driven out of Mecca for his attempts to establish Islamic monotheism. He fled to Medina, where he was in constant dialogue with the local Jewish community. There are even indications that he attempted to persuade his Jewish fellow citizens to support a "fusion" of Jewish traditions with the new revelation of the Koran. For example, he suggested designating Jerusalem as the new "navel of the world" instead of Mecca.

During our trip, we were also reminded of Jacobello del Fiore, an early Renaissance painter and mystic who devised criteria for assessing the level of development of religions. He distinguished three stages, which he named after the three members of the Holy Trinity. The Age of the Father was followed by the Age of the Son, which is succeeded by the Age of the Holy Spirit. Here is how I translate these ages into the language we have been using in attempting to understand religion as an instrument of reconnection:

- IN THE FATHER STAGE, the divine is recognized as the all-encompassing wholeness of energy, love, and consciousness that guides and sustains the universe. Eternity is its distinguishing characteristic. It is communicated to human beings through the visions and messages of prophets and saints. In the figure of the Redeemer, this all-encompassing wholeness is even capable of appearing among humans. Relating to the Father takes the form of worship or adoration.

- THE SON STAGE is a phase of individuation. It results from the insight that all-encompassing divinity not only pervades the universe but can also be realized by each human individual in his or her own being. In the Son phase, individuals are called upon to seek the divine within by following their own inspiration and obeying their own sense of responsibility. The way of the Son is the individual path to self-knowledge and charitable love.
- THE STAGE OF THE HOLY SPIRIT stands for the intricate ways in which the quality of divine wholeness manifests in daily life. The divinity is not only worshiped (as in the Father phase) or personally embodied by individuals (as in the Son phase). Now the all-encompassing divinity—all the energy, love, and consciousness of eternity—begins to pervade societal institutions, interpersonal relationships, and the community of all beings. There is no longer any need for specifically religious activity.

Under the influence of the rigid structures of linear thinking, Jacobello del Fiore saw the Jewish religion as the Kingdom of the Father, the bygone era of divine revelation, while the present and its prevailing Christianity corresponded to the Kingdom of the Son. Del Fiore reserved the "third kingdom" of the Holy Spirit for the future. Some people see it as the dawning of the Aquarian Age, while others believe the concept was used in a blasphemous attempt to legitimize the Nazi's Third Reich.

From the perspective of reconnection, none of the three stages of modern religion is less valuable than others; none belongs either to the outdated past or to the uncertain future. All three phases are equally important, yet each one has its own profound meaning if lived in the present—that is, here and now. Why shouldn't we worship the all-encompassing divinity—regardless of whether we call it Allah or Yahweh—while the individual "I" simultaneously embodies the divine qualities of personal responsibility, free creativity, and undogmatic thinking?

I would go so far as to assert that the three religions founded in succession in Near East, the world's navel, embody the three fundamental stages of human reconnection. Since spending time in that part of the world in April 2001, I have become deeply convinced that these religions were founded to initiate us, as human individuals, into the three successive phases of reconnection, to free us from our existential alienation and to lead us home:

- JUDAISM STANDS FOR THE "FATHER STAGE," which can be equated with collective reconnection to the primal source of all being. This source is given different names by different religions—Jehovah, God the Father, or Allah—but its unique identity remains the same. It speaks to us from the Holy Scriptures of all three religions, inviting us to connect with its wholeness. Tuning in to the primal source of all being, whether through rituals, prayer, or contemplation, is the uncontested basis of the reconnection process fostered by all three religions.
- CHRISTIANITY STANDS FOR THE "SON STAGE." In this second phase, individuals learn to be independent, to listen to the voice within, to make decisions based on individual core values, and to live responsibly in freedom. The ties that bind us to a particular race, ethnic group, or religion become less important. As individuals, we are challenged to stand on our own two feet and to connect with spiritual or religious communities of our own choosing. Although usually contested by all three religions, the individual's right to pursue an individual spiritual path without association with any religious institution is the basis for the second phase of reconnection.
- ISLAM STANDS FOR THE "STAGE OF THE HOLY SPIRIT," the phase in which divine virtues and human visions of peace become a reality in daily life. Islam's creation of a unitary, all-pervasive energy field hints at archetypal intentions for the third phase of reconnection, namely, to create and maintain—consciously, lovingly, in common, and in harmony with the universe—the energy field of a harmonious civilization that allows all beings, human and nonhuman, to live peacefully, creatively, and happily.

Each of these three religions was called into existence to foster, in its own way, the reconnection of modern human beings to the divine. Is it possible to see this fact as the common nucleus of the religions of the Near East? All three devote themselves to embedding us anew in the cosmic whole. To help us sense and foster their commonalities within ourselves, I suggest the following meditation:

Meditation

- Connect with the bowl of the Earth beneath you and the dome of heaven above. Imagine the Earth's forces rising through you to heaven in a spiral, while heaven's forces descend through you in the form of a column of light that sinks deep into the earth. Sense this exchange within yourself. (Judaism)
- Then imagine that the flow of forces is consciously intercepted by the crystal in the center of your heart, making it shine and radiate. Its rays reach far into your surroundings, loving and blessing all the beings of life around you. (Christianity)
- Now link the forces and beings of all-encompassing life together with delicate strands of light, centering the network on a point behind your navel. Sense yourself in the middle of the network that connects all with all. Breathe together with the whole. (Islam)
- Attempt to sense all three qualities simultaneously in order to hear who the quintessential human being is/what it means to be truly human.

The Role of the Goddess

Isn't this a wonderful meditative experience of the harmony of the three phases of reconnection initiated by Judaism, Christianity, and Islam? And what a shame it is that mistrust, enmity, and war repeatedly develop between individuals or communities belonging to these three related religions! All three, each in its own way, were intended to advance the process of regaining our wholeness. Instead, they only separate and isolate individuals from each other. It is painful to be forced to watch the growing discrepancy between the spiritual origin of these religions and current political realities.

Our group encountered one of the worst causes of this discrepancy at St. Catherine's Monastery at the foot of Mount Sinai. As I mentioned earlier, my daughter and colleague Ana was able to locate the great heart-center for all of Sinai, thanks to a message from the angelic world. As the group was tuning in to the place, Ana and I clashed. The brief but pointed disagreement was painful for all of us. Significantly, it took place in the sacred domain of the heart-center.

Only later, in studying the traditional accounts of what happened near Mount Sinai after the Israelites escaped from bondage in Egypt, were we able to understand the cause of our conflict. This disagreement between myself and my closest colleague, my own daughter, reflected the energy pattern of a traumatic conflict in the long-ago epoch of the Exodus. On their flight from Egypt, the Jews were led by two brothers, Aaron and Moses. As the Bible confirms (Exodus 4: 14–16), both brothers were appointed through divine guidance to lead the Jews to the Promised Land. Nonetheless, the brothers came into conflict in the famous episode at the foot of Mount Sinai. While Moses was spending forty days praying on the mountain, after which he received the Ten Commandments from God's own hand, Aaron was collecting gold and silver to forge a calf to be worshiped as a divinity in the traditional fertility rites. When Moses came down the mountain with the tables of the law and saw the people dancing around the golden calf, he lost his temper and smashed the tables.

Actually, if he had obeyed the Ten Commandments he held in his hands, he should not have been so quick to condemn the collective dancing around the golden calf as sinful. It is important to note that both of these actions were carried out by brothers whom God had chosen to lead his people, but it is also impossible to overlook the fact that the forms they chose for expressing connection to the divine are in fact opposites. The views that collided at the foot of Mount Sinai reflect two completely different aspects of divine revelation.

The veiled symbol of dancing around the golden calf undoubtedly refers to a fertility ritual honoring the Goddess. But who is the Goddess? She was not mentioned in our threefold subdivision of the religious process, but she represents the female aspect of the divine. Does this have nothing to do with religion, or have we been overlooking a decisive aspect of reality?

We have not been overlooking it. As we traveled in our imagination from the Sphinx and the Giza plateau through Sinai and all of Israel, we were familiarizing ourselves with the body of the Goddess. We were led through the most intimate parts of her landscape temple. We experienced her broad white back, smelled the fragrance of her genitals, and listened to the pulsing of her heart. She presented us with wonderful colors, odors, and vistas. We were sensing the life-body of the Goddess from the inside.

And then the presence of the Goddess disappeared as we began to concern ourselves with the three religions of Judaism, Christianity, and Islam. For several millennia, they have determined the fate of the Near East (and even that of the entire Earth) in the name of God. The stone tables that Moses smashed represent the commandments of the male God, not those of the Goddess.

A Goddess religion never existed, could never exist. The Goddess stands for the universal web of life and love of which we are part from eternity to eternity. Why would we need to know anything about religion or "reconnection" for that? In her creative phase, the Goddess represents all possible instruments of the creative act. She deals with the joy of embodiment, with life as it manifests in all of its different expressions. We humans and our culture represent only one facet of life's abundance, which also includes the landscape, the Earth's natural world, and the entire manifest universe. When we are already part of something, we do not need to "reconnect" with it.

But don't the spoiled fruits of freedom, our misdeeds and violence, cry out for forgiveness, redemption, and reconnection? The Goddess has a clear answer: transformation. We humans are exposed to experiences that allow us to recognize our strayings from the path as such, so that through transformation, we may regain our place in the fabric of the whole. This takes much time, patience, and forgiveness; it does not need religion.

But what does Moses stand for, along with the tables of the law that he received from the hand of God? The Ten Commandments were given to him to prevent wrongdoing and to teach people how to act ethically. Here, we are not dealing with a female principle that works from within (and thus has no interest in religious endeavors). Instead, we are dealing with male energy, whose nature it is to act from a distance, "from outside," as it were. The result is the emergence of a fascinating free space for independent decision-making that allows individuals and cultures to be creative.

A simultaneous consequence, however, is the inevitable separation that results from subjective-objective distancing in any patriarchally inspired culture. This distancing soon leads to social stratification and contradictory interests, and its ultimate consequence is war. The cosmos threatens to break apart, and as a next step a variety of different religions are established to bridge the divide that threatens to develop.

If we compare the female and male cosmic principles, we find that these two aspects of the divine are highly complementary. If they are denied the opportunity to complement each other, however, aberrations are unavoidable. This is exactly what happened in the traumatic incident at the foot of Mount Sinai when the people who revived the Goddess fertility rites were dealt a bloody punishment. The tables of the Ten Commandments—representing all three religions of the Near East—became the symbol of the emerging patriarchal culture.

Presumably, a whole series of such clashes occurred before the connection to the female aspect of the divine as well as to the Goddess of the individual landscape became taboo. The total dominance of monotheism produced a discrepancy between religious goals and real life. The fact that the founders of the three religious had the best of intentions and faithfully obeyed the words of their God helped little. Aberrations were still inevitable.

In the absence of the Goddess, we lose control over whether or not a given ideology or procedure is in harmony with the heart-impulse that called it into being. The truthfulness of specific actions and trains of thought can be recognized only by experiencing their effects on our own bodies or other human or natural bodies. Trickery and deceit find their way into the fabric of divine revelation with the help of reason, magic, or the hunger for power, but when confronted by the Goddess, by manifest life, they lose their energy and power.

Striving to Transform the Religious Energy Field

On April 24, 2001, our last day before leaving for home, our group expressed the desire to bring closure to the theme of reconnection. We were in Jerusalem, and we realized that we were standing on a hilltop sacred to all three religions. It would be easy for Jerusalem to serve as a place of reconciliation. Tragically, however, this place has been a source of conflicts and bloody religious wars for hundreds of years.

As we walked through Jerusalem, our geomantically trained eyes could not fail to notice that the religious activities of Jews, Muslims, and Christians had been concentrated for centuries on two rocks that once crowned the hill of Jerusalem. In the course of history, they have either been destroyed by religious zealots or completely built up with shrines, so to outer perception they are no longer recognizable as rocks today. Jews pray beneath the summit of Mount Moriah, which was once the site of the Temple of Solomon, the symbol of their covenant with God. This cliff is also the third most holy place in the Muslim world. According to tradition, it is where Mohammed ascended into heaven, and it is now the site of the impressive mosque of the Dome of the Rock. Jerusalem's second holy rock once stood outside the city walls. This is the hill of Golgotha, where Jesus Christ was crucified in the prelude to the Resurrection, the central mystery of the Christian faith. The hill itself was leveled by Muslim conquerors in the Middle Ages. Today it has been replaced by an impressive array of Coptic, Orthodox, Catholic, and Protestant churches around the Holy Grave.

To experience the energetic quality of the Temple Mount, our group proceeded to the tunnel dug by archeologists along the foundations of Solomon's Temple. Underground, we were quite close to the cliff that the two hostile religions of Palestine hold most sacred. In that underground passageway, as in all the significant places we visited, we intoned an intense, ringing song to send healing impulses to the place. Earlier, as we were still concentrating in silence on the rock, I saw that its energies were unimaginably deeply anchored in the earth. Inside it, however, I perceived to my horror a gigantic black sphere in which forces and beings circled endlessly, trapped by an evil spell and searching in vain for a way out. In their tragic revolutions, I sensed the countless injuries and traumas that had been accumulating for centuries in the emotional atmosphere of the place.

The next instant, I was shaken by a call to open my heart to the cosmic extensions of the temple rock. I barely had time to tune in to the appropriate layer when I perceived a bundle of blindingly white energy hanging in the heavens. Originally, the fusion of the bundle of light from above and the life-giving energy of the cliff below must have triggered an explosion of light. Today, these two energy sources appeared to be separated from each other.

Later, to experience the actual rock of the hill of Golgotha, we descended two stories deep into the lowest crypt of the Church of the Holy Sepulcher. The crypt is carved into the subterranean remnants of the hill of Golgotha. Standing there, we stood in the center of the former hill, very close to the Jerusalem heart-center that beats within the rock of Golgotha, according to Ana's angelic message. There we sang again to offer the heart-center an impulse for renewal. While we were intoning, I was granted an insight. The cliff began to vibrate from within as an intense transformation took place. It broke open and its receptivity to the cosmic light descending from above was restored. Finally, the cliff's energy field was transformed into a black, fragrant rose, and a sense of relief spread out around it. I had no doubt that I had been allowed to behold a vision of the future healing of the place.

When we finished singing, we worked on visualizing a lemniscate that united the two holy hills, with one loop of the horizontal figure eight running through the Temple Mount, the other through Golgotha. After concentrating for some time on visualizing the lemniscate, I noticed that its crossing point slowly moved to coincide with my own heart-center. Since several other participants had the same experience, we interpreted it as a key to stimulating the transformation of the three related yet antagonistic religious fields. This key has two complementary faces. One has to do with the fact that the lemniscate's crossing point positioned itself inside the human being. Although the loops connect the two rocks of the Jerusalem landscape, their junction is to be found in the center of human hearts. In other words, a lasting solution to a problem that is almost exclusively considered to be worldly or political in character must be sought first within individuals.

The centering of the lemniscate in the middle of the heart also seems to mean that heart-qualities play a decisive role in transforming the shadow aspect of religious energy fields. This is the second face. Ordinarily, we are much too quick to equate heart-energy with outpourings of love. Love can indeed flow into the world through the heart-center, where a source of a special sort is located. This source comes about through the simultaneous conflict and mutual attraction (harmony) of forces and qualities that are such opposites that they actually shouldn't have anything to do with each other. Through the "harmony of opposites," however, the enormous potential energy that we call "love" comes about.

If love is recognized not merely as a romantic emotion but as a force capable of making peace arise from conflict, it is truly the key that is needed in the conflict-dominated situation in the Near East. The best way to experience what this actually means is through a guided mediation in which the two great opposites of life and death are "married" in the center of the heart. In this meditation, Golgotha, the hill of the Crucifixion, stands for death and the Temple Mount, site of Mohammed's ascent into heaven, stands for the forces of life. Transposed to the human body, the quality of life is to be sought in the light-filled space in front of the chest, the quality of eternity (which can reasonably be associated with death) in the space behind the back.

Meditation

- Sit quietly for a while, concentrating on your heart-center.
- Imagine going as far as you possibly can into the space in front of you. Then return in an arc to the middle of your heart. Repeat this several times. (Quality of the Temple Mount)
- Now expand in your imagination into the space behind your back, as far as you possibly can. Return again in an arc to the middle of your heart. Repeat this several times. (Quality of the hill of Golgotha)
- Now push the space you moved through behind your back forward, in the direction of embodied life. Push the space in front of your chest backward, in the direction of eternity.
- As you do so, pay attention to the energy or quality that is born in the middle of your heart. Hold on to this quality for a while, then let it radiate out into the world that longs for healing. Don't forget Israel/Palestine, the myth-enshrouded world-navel.
- Imagine yourself standing in the center of the Holy Land and sending your love out from that point. The circular waves of your love are bestowed on the energy field of the entire Earth and bathe all beings.

Foundations of a Holistic Peace Project in Israel/Palestine

A Disturbing Dream-Message

After our pilgrimage was over, on April 24, 2001, our last night in Jerusalem, I had a dream that impressed me deeply and offered suggestions on how to continue the healing project in Israel/Palestine that we had began with our trip. I was standing in a long row of people who were all waiting patiently to be executed. We all seemed to accept impending decapitation as something totally normal. As we drew closer to the place of execution, I realized to my astonishment that the executioner was a woman. She was unusually tall, and her face with its very masculine features conveyed her unwavering determination to complete this bloody work. And in fact the process was running so smoothly that the person in front of me was already laying his head on the block. But something went wrong with this execution, and the female executioner was forced to repeat the stroke. Even on the second attempt, the axe hit the person's skull instead of his neck. The most shocking thing about all this was that I knew the person well. He was one of my closest colleagues.

This dramatic incident sounded a warning signal in my ears, and a question flared up in my mind: How would my wife and my daughters take the news of my senseless execution? This sobering thought triggered vehement resistance in me, tearing me away from the execution scene and thus awakening me from the dream.

It was too soon to decode the dream's message in its entirety. I was simply speechless. Only much later, during preparations for continuing our healing project in 2002, was I able to recognize a few practical tips on how to proceed in approaching the problem of peace in the Holy Land from an unusual and completely different perspective.

The invitation to continue the project had come spontaneously during our trip when I gave a lecture at the Waldorf School of Kiryat Tivon and reported on our experiences and intentions. When I took up the invitation and arrived in Tel Aviv in spring of 2002, I was surprised to hear that almost fifty people from all over Israel had signed up to spend an entire week developing the healing project with me. We spent the first three days in Jerusalem. On March 20, when the workshop began, the weather suddenly turned as cold as winter again. A strong wind raged, occasionally interrupted by heavy rainfall, and yet there were brief interludes when the sun broke through the clouds in full force. In contrast, the next four days, which we spent in Galilee, were sunny and calm.

Meanwhile, the political situation in Israel/Palestine had intensified to such an extent that the message of my shattering dream about the female executioner was easier to decode. I interpreted the abortive attempt at beheading the victim in front of me as a sign of a decisive turning point in the course of the crisis. No change was outwardly visible as yet; on the contrary, things were only getting worse. Nonetheless, the dream suggested that an opportunity to reverse course on the road to hell was now present, buried deep within the current world situation. The decision that would make this reversal possible seemed to lie with individuals capable of inwardly recognizing the decisive moment.

Dramatic signs of an impending reversal—corresponding to the failed execution in my dream—were emerging in the Holy Land in the spring of 2002 even though the situation seemed unpromising, even hopeless, due to Palestinian suicide attacks on Israeli soil and incursions by the Israeli army into the Palestinian autonomous territories.

Based on the message of my dream, I see two insights as relevant to continuing our healing initiatives in Israel/Palestine:

- Catastrophic perversion of the female principle is one of the leading causes of the persistent, repetitive violence in the Near East.
- The consciousness of the regional cultures lacks any feeling for the present.

Perversion of the Female Principle

In previous sections on the geomantic dimensions of our trip from the Pyramids across Sinai to Jerusalem, I have already discussed the centuries-old domination of the patriarchal systems that suppress the holistic female quality in Israel/Palestine. But the first part of my dream-message brought to light a shattering aspect of the problem that I had previously overlooked, namely, suppression of the female principle to the point of perversion. In Israel/Palestine today, female energies are denying their own character to become instruments of patterns of violence. This is why the role of the executioner in my dream was played by a woman with male features.

The female character of the violence is evident, for example, in the fact that no actual war is being waged in spite of the grave conflicts of recent years. On the Palestinian side, the struggle is often led by a resistance movement of rebellious adolescents. Also death is being sown in places where innocent people congregate daily, such as marketplaces or public transport. The Israeli army, meanwhile, focuses more on applying psychological pressure to the Palestinians (through revenge, debasement, and inciting fear) than on "classical" martial skirmishes.

In reality, therefore, we can say that both sides are waging a war that uses perversion of female qualities as a weapon. Places of life are transformed into places of death; adolescents are seduced into acting out the conflicts of adult males. The emotional energy field, instead of serving as a gentle counterbalance to prevailing rigid forms of thought, becomes a battleground.

As individuals scattered throughout the world who take the fate of the Holy Land to heart, can we do anything about this situation? Or must we watch helplessly as misused female forces do battle with life's abundance? I see two possibilities here. Within our individual energy fields, we can each pay more attention to inner balance and ensure that the female aspect of our own being is allowed to express itself without falsification. This strengthens the Goddess's worldwide network of life.

The other possibility would be direct work in Israel/Palestine with the goal of drawing attention to the country's fundamental qualities instead of to the political struggle for power and its perverted "female" violence. Female energies will be able to have healing effects on the current situation if their unique, unadulterated character is recognized and no longer overwhelmed by the dominant culture. Female energies embody the great potential of unspoiled forces of love and life that lie dormant in the depths of the countryside and in human hearts. I believe that these concealed energies, if awakened, would be capable of revolutionizing the national situation so that a path to peace would become clear.

A couple of my experiences in the Jerusalem seminar of March 2002 suggest the kinds of energies and qualities I've been talking about. At that time, our efforts focused on discovering and reviving certain places in the city where it is easiest to access the Goddess of the place (avoiding the more masculine-sounding term "spirit of the place"). These locations are geomantic focal points in various layers of space. They provide a basis for communicating with the Goddess—meaning in this case the soul of the universe, of which both the soul of Jerusalem and the Earth Soul are holographic fragments.

The site farthest from the city center is a source of primal energy that flows up from great depths. It is located in the Jerusalem Forest in the Nahal Revadim valley on the city's western edge. I also perceived the source as a gate to the underworld through which the soul of Jerusalem retreats to gather up its forces in silence. Conversely, a shortcut of sorts leads from the source to the Old City, allowing the soul of the place to reach Jerusalem in quiet moments to spread its blessing over the city landscape. The shortcut, which resembles a channel of light, leads between the Knesset and the National Court to the Old City.

In the park's most distant corner, in front of the National Court, lies a point where the city's elemental consciousness is focused and fans out, binding the entire space together in a fabric as of fine golden threads. From this point, the earth's sexual energy spreads out in waves to stimulate abundant life and (to the extent possible) restore the paradisiacal quality of the landscape.

In a vision that came to me in this place, the huge head of the Goddess, large as the entire city, sank into the depths of the landscape and then gradually rose above the surface again. I noticed then for the first time that the top of her skull was open. In place of the brain, the hills of Jerusalem were nestled with their countless buildings of pinkish Jerusalem limestone, interspersed with mighty trees rustling in the breeze.

I recognized another "retreat" from which the soul of the city can work in the Mamilla Pool, a huge artificial basin that now lies empty but was formerly used to supply the Old City with drinking water. As I perceived it, the empty space of the pool where rainwater was once collected is now filled with an invisible etheric temple. There is almost no other place in Jerusalem where the presence of the angels of Earth and Heaven can be sensed so clearly. This forgotten pool offers the soul of the universe more space than any of the City's famous sacred sites.

The Power of the Past

The second cause of the ever-repeating conflicts in the Near East is related to a behavior pattern that is best described as "absence of the present." In my dramatic dream, the lurking danger of the absent present was represented by the crowd's acceptance of execution as something quite normal. Individuals embedded in the fixed idea that reality is inescapable fact, predetermined since biblical times, succumb to the consequences of their own pattern of behavior and become its victims.

In the imagery of my dream, salvation approached as soon as I recalled my responsibility to life in the body by asking myself what my wife and children would say when they heard that I had voluntarily allowed myself to be beheaded in a distant land. Direct, bodily connection to the reality of the moment reinstated the present in full force, restored my capacity to make independent decisions, and erased the dominance of the past along with all of the fixed ideas and entrenched traditions that had squashed the potency and expansion of contemporary currents of life. A lasting healing process could begin.

In geomantic terms, the absence of the present in the Holy Land is evident in the specific historical roles and religious meanings that are attributed to all of the country's individual foci of life-energy. Quite possibly, no one ever wonders about their current role in relationship to the country's energy-organism. The relative importance of places is determined not by their actual geomantic function within the landscape as a whole (that is, within the holon of Israel or of the Earth) but by the role they (presumably) played in the past, according to accounts in the Bible or the Koran. As tourists, we are told all possible details of the biblical past and sometimes even about the prophesied future of a place but never about its actual, true identity. As a consequence, the countryside and its individual places are locked into a religious or ideological duality of past and present and thus kept in a state of permanent alienation.

The connection to reality in the here and now is completely missing. This ungroundedness presents infinite opportunities to manipulate the land and its human occupants and to force them against their will into seemingly dead-end situations. But because the way the country's residents think and live is the cause of this flight into the past and/or future, their predicament is actually a case of self-manipulation.

To initiate healing in this almost hopeless situation, a different attitude toward life and landscape should be developed. We must first ask about the wellbeing of specific ethnic groups, individuals, or places without reference to preconceived ideas or ideological norms. Next, we must find simple ways of transforming the unfortunate present situation into abundance of life.

Grounding is needed at every moment and in every place in the Near East to allow reality to shine out in full force with its inherent potential for peace. We saw one example of a "grounded" way of acting that does justice to the complexity of the present in the Sekem Community in the Nile Delta, which has wrested huge expanses of farmland from the desert and combines biodynamic agriculture with public welfare projects and educational and cultural opportunities for the community's many coworkers. For our tour group, visiting Sekem was a welcome change of pace—a place in the Near East that does not reflect the impact of ancient historical, religious, and political burdens but functions in the present and is anchored in modern spiritual endeavors. In Sekem, it is possible to perceive the original richness of Egypt's field of life-energy, the luxuriant etheric world that is otherwise suppressed by the above-mentioned disruptive factors and banished to the netherworld. We were deeply moved by the beauty and energy of the etheric extension of space, which ancient Egyptian culture surely must have cultivated consciously. We perceived Sekem as a welcome opening through which currently exiled qualities of space may once again manifest freely in the present.

Trapped in the Void between Inhaling and Exhaling

A second dream alerted me to an additional problem in the Holy Land. I dreamed I was holding two watches. One watch belonged to someone else, who had asked me to keep it for him at some point in the past. Now it was time to give it back. When I took it off the shelf, I was holding my own watch in the same hand. At that point, I noticed that the other person's watch seemed to be measuring a very different sort of time than my own. Its face was black and divided into different fields that held little illuminated circles with unfamiliar numbers and many hands.

All this took place in a bathroom. As I held both watches in my left hand and attempted to fasten my own watch to my right wrist, I was standing very close to a deep toilet chute, and exactly what I had feared the previous moment happened: The watch with the strange dial slipped out of my hand and disappeared down the deep, narrow chute.

Aghast, I followed its fall with my eyes. Who could possibly get it back up out of that pit? But then I noticed that the chute was not a toilet but a complicated time tunnel made of fine plates of stainless steel with a matte finish. Individual periods or epochs of time were separated by circular segments made of similar plates. The mysterious watch fell through two time-segments and got caught on the third. At that moment I became aware that the dream's secret message lay in the relationship between the watch in my hand and the other one glinting far below me in the time tunnel.

At first this dream reminded me of an eerie experience I had in Jerusalem: I got the distinct impression that the Holy Land had lost its breath. In my inner perception, I sensed that the country was trapped in the standstill between inhaling and exhaling. This situation felt extremely threatening. How long can a country and all its natural kingdoms survive in the empty space between a long-gone epoch of inhalation and an exhalation stage that had not yet begun?

I equated the past epoch of inhalation with the mysterious watch from my dream, stuck two stories below me in the time tunnel. This watch represented a distant epoch of revelation when the path to reconnection was proclaimed to human beings through the words of the biblical Prophets, the Gospels, or the Koran. Unbelievable spiritual energies lay in these three waves of past revelation.

The wave of spiritual revelation in the Near East, which gave human beings a completely new inspiration to reconnect with the heavens and the Earth, is long since over. On the other hand, the Near East no longer has any feeling for the Holy Land's inherent potency, which would allow forces of inspiration to be breathed out into the fabric of society, into interpersonal relationships, etc. Rigid religious ideas, military conflicts, and forced poverty have long since reduced this potency to fragments.I associated the exhalation still to come with the second watch, which I was trying unsuccessfully to put on in my dream when the other one fell into the time tunnel. The absence of exhalation relates to the problem of the "absence of the present," which I mentioned previously. The second watch was meant to show me, a representative of modern humankind, the real time of the current moment.

The Holy Land today is in a dramatic situation, trapped in the empty space between inhaling and exhaling. During my lecture at the Waldorf School in Kiryat Tivon, the landscape itself spoke to this situation in its own language. While I was telling about our trip, my gaze was drawn as if by magic through the window across from me to a perfectly round hillock on the edge of Mount Carmel. A cosmographic character suddenly appeared, floating above the summit of the little hill.

One year later, in the spring of 2002, I finally had an opportunity to climb the hill that had spoken to me so insistently. A geomantic examination of its summit confirmed that this was a place of connection between heaven and Earth, a "larynx" for the surrounding landscape. The character that had floated above informed me that in the distant past, this place allowed seers and prophets to converse with the spiritual world and played an important role in the wave of revelation in that distant epoch of inhalation.

Unfortunately, it was also obvious that this very quality led to misuse of the summit's energy in a later era. As a consequence, it is now completely blocked. Meanwhile, the hill has been completely denuded of trees and now is enduring further misuse as a racecourse for ATVs. Like many other holy places, it is suspended in the void between the long-gone inhalation of revelation and the desperately needed stage of exhalation, which is slipping ever further into the uncertain future as destruction continues in the present.

Blockage of the Spiritual World

While preparing for my seminar in Jerusalem in the spring of 2002, in the Rose Park (between the Israeli parliament and the National Court), I discovered a place where the presence of the dead can be felt. This discovery highlighted a second theme that is almost totally hushed up today, namely, the potential for valuable exchange between the world of the living and the world of the dead.

One year earlier, at the Pyramids, I had asked my inner master why the Egyptians had devoted so much energy, attention, and artistry to life after death. The answer was that in this way, Egyptian culture had made important adaptations to the subtle etheric world where the dead tarried. By embalming corpses, artistically embellishing their burial chambers, and richly equipping the deceased for the afterlife, the Egyptians made it possible for the souls of the dead to linger long after death in the Earth's near-material, etheric spaces, thus facilitating communication between the dead and the living. The resulting etheric "niches" allowed the dead to contact the living.

I am not talking here about questionable communication with the lost souls imprisoned between worlds, who need help from the living and from the angels to find their place in the divine order of the universe again. Rather, I am talking only about those departed souls who are sufficiently advanced in their personal development to freely offer help to human society during times of need. On the one hand, these souls have access to universal knowledge, but they have also accumulated a rich store of life experience in the human world and have learned how to avoid traps on the path of personal development. Their advice might help solve the present problems in Israel/Palestine. At no time have the words or assistance of the wise individuals who appeared as prophets throughout history been more needed than now.

During our group's visit to the basilica on Mount Tabor, I discovered a wonderful location for communication between the two worlds. To my inner vision, the mountain initially appeared to be split into two almost completely separate halves. One half was dull and chaotic, the other clear as a quartz crystal. In my consciousness, I slid through the clear half and found myself deep inside the mountain. Looking around, I found myself surrounded by the souls of the dead. I was reminded of Gospel accounts of

Jesus communicating with his spiritual forebears on Mount Tabor. Meanwhile, our group had begun to sing in spontaneous harmony in the basilica's choir loft. The vibrating tones enabled me to continue my observations successfully. The obscured half of the space became clearer and more structured, and I noticed that the mountain's pyramidal form was reflected in the sky. The overall image resembled an hourglass, with the physical mountain below reflected in the etheric mountain "hanging" above it. The summit of Mount Tabor, dominated by the basilica, was like a link between the spiritual and earthly worlds.

Within the fabric of Israel/Palestine as a whole, therefore, Mount Tabor could serve as a corridor for communication between the physically embodied half of the world on the one hand and the world of the heavens on the other. If this corridor is intact, it could be used to conduct conversations with the spiritual world.

Freeing the Country's Life Forces

We experienced Timna Park, located in the southern part of Israel, as an extensive landscape temple that has not yet been completely explored. This time, we concentrated on its center, the site of Solomon's Pillars. The ancient Egyptians partially transformed this massive rock formation into a temple of the goddess Hathor. I understood the rock formation as an etheric womb of sorts that allowed the creative word of the Goddess to be revealed, bestowing fertility on the land. This function corresponds to the life-giving role we had recognized in the landscape temple of Israel/Palestine in nearby Elat, on the Red Sea.

The "Goddess," however, means not only cow-faced Hathor but also the universal quality she embodies within the Egyptian pantheon—that is, the World Soul's ability to constantly produce the life forces that maintain the land's fertility. In this sense, the Goddess (as the complement of God) is the source of life-energy, love, and the immortal dance of life.

The World Soul would not be able to fill the landscape with abundant life, however, if the geomantic organism of the place did not permit exchanges between cosmic and earthly manifestations of being. In certain special places such as Solomon's Pillars, space "turns inside out" and transphysical dimensions can be accessed in an instant. Conversely, this inversion of space also allows the Earth's creative forces to be fructified again and again by cosmic forces.

The cosmic and earthly aspects of the Goddess work together in the desert of the Timna landscape temple to make the land fertile. The surrounding mountains and rock formations work like a sounding body, amplifying the message of the Goddess's creative word so it can be "heard" throughout the larger region.

As I was tuning in to the temple of Hathor at Solomon's Pillars, the Goddess appeared to me as a fragrant presence. She called on me to hold my hands in front of my face in a specific position and to breathe through them. I knew intuitively that she was attempting to initiate me into a form of communication that could restore the dialogue between heaven and earth. Without the active cooperation of human beings, who control the land and make decisions about how it is used, the creative word of the Goddess, which maintains the fertility of the landscape, is condemned to silence. At one time, Hathor's temple at the foot of Solomon's Pillars did indeed serve this fertility-renewing function. Today, however, no one makes the effort any more to maintain the fruitful conversation between the heavens, the earth, and human beings. But through the holographic exercise the Goddess showed me, this life-giving dialogue can be restored. The Hathor gesture, which allows us to initiate a conversation with creation (or at least a particular aspect of it), can be applied anywhere.

The Hathor Gesture

- With your hands, make a pyramid with its tip level with your third eye.
- In this position, your two thumbs will be right in front of your mouth, easy for your lips to touch. Leave a small gap open between your thumbs for your breath to flow through.
- Consciously and with sensitivity, take several breaths through the channel between your thumbs to enliven the pyramid with your breath.
- Now you can inaudibly whisper the message you want to send into the world of the invisible. (For example, you can tell a specific tree or even all of creation that you love it.) Through the contact between your lips and the tips of your thumbs, the message also becomes audible for those who have no physical ears.
- In conclusion, place your hands in your lap and immerse yourself in the space that manifested during this meditation.

A complementary aspect of Timna's energy of creation is embodied in Mount Carmel in the northwestern part of Israel. I recognized the summit of the mountain, near the famous Carmelite monastery, as a conduit for forces that give material form to etheric life. At work here is the wisdom of embodiment, the feminine knowledge of giving birth into the world of matter. The primal energies of this mountain revealed themselves to me as sexual forces. The symbols I saw suggest that the summit has been sacred to the Virgin Goddess, the keeper of the mysteries of menstruation and birth, from time immemorial.

If the landscape temple of Timna Park is dedicated to the Goddess's creative word, which initiates the land into the quality of life, Mount Carmel stands for life forces that transform this creative word into the various manifestations and currents of embodied life. If Timna corresponds to the larynx, then Carmel is a mighty womb. And in fact the worldwide movement of Carmelite monasteries, which began here, is dedicated to Mary, the Virgin Mother.

But what am I attempting to say by describing my encounters with the female aspect of the divine and its holy sites in Israel/Palestine? To introduce healing processes in the Near East, we must draw public attention to the country's living reality. Today, however, public attention is focused almost exclusively on the catastrophic political situation, which is the subject of constant media commentary and broadcast throughout the world. Our gaze, held spellbound by the bloody knots of conflict, must be released from this suicidal lethargy. The antidote to political rigidity, the force that will set us free, lies in the radiant presence of life, which corresponds to the love-energy in the human being's essential core.

Dominance of Rigid Thought Patterns and Dogmas

Another possible thread of healing in the Holy Land has to do with breaking down the rigidified mental images, spiritual dogmas, and patterns of feeling and thinking that took root long ago in the souls of the two antagonistic ethnic groups as a consequence of historical, philosophical, or religious developments. Almost without being noticed, they now influence current connections between Israelis and Palestinians and prevent a peaceful solution.

We might call such patterns "perverted archetypes." Although rooted in divinely inspired ideas, they have been misunderstood, perverted, and ultimately applied for negative purposes as they evolved through history. Divinely perfect archetypes developed into perverted dogmas that now negatively influence the further development of communities or ethnic groups on subconscious levels. This influence and the associated destructive alignment of life-currents can be eliminated only by restoring the perverted archetype to its positive form.

One such thought pattern is the concept of the "promised land," the idea that divine revelation granted the Jewish people authority over Israel/Palestine. According to this idea, the Jews were allowed to occupy the Promised Land in God's name, without any regard for its indigenous occupants. In the twentieth century, this pattern was repeated and an almost identical situation developed, but this time the local inhabitants were not the Canaanites of biblical times but Arabic-speaking Palestinians. The words of the Bible that best characterize the tragedy of this perverted archetype are: "And the LORD spake unto Moses in the plains of Moab by Jordan near Jericho, saying, Speak unto the children of Israel, and say unto them, When ye are passed over Jordan into the land of Canaan; then ye shall drive out all the inhabitants of the land from before you, and destroy all their pictures, and destroy all their molten images, and quite pluck down all their high places: and ye shall dispossess the inhabitants *of* the land, and dwell therein: for I have given you the land to possess it" (Numbers 33: 50–53). It is hard to believe that such words are part of divine revelation. We resist them with all our being. Could they possibly be a misinterpretation of divine intent? On the basis of our geomantic decoding of the Holy Land, it certainly seems justified to ask whether the divine decision to resettle the Jewish people in the Promised Land might not be understood completely differently today. The result would be a completely different responsibility to the land and its original owners.

But what if the term "promised land" meant the ability of the landscape of Israel/Palestine to reflect and reveal the essence of the human being in its wholeness? What if it meant the "promised land" of reconnection, of becoming truly human? It was exactly this ability of the Holy Land that permitted both a new, direct covenant between God and humans and the first embodiment of God's precious qualities on Earth. What if the Jews of those times were actually assigned the task of restoring the connection to the divine on behalf of all of us? They would have had to settle the area between the Red Sea and the Sea of Galilee, which may have been the only landscape capable of supporting such reconnection at that time.

Since then, the religious values of reconnection have been further developed and carried throughout the world by Christianity, Islam, and Judaism itself. They no longer need the Holy Land for their actualization. By now, human beings are meant to have learned how to cultivate the qualities of universal connectedness within themselves, regardless of where they live. If in spite of the wonderful fruits of this further development, we in the twenty-first century still insist on an interpretation that is three thousand years old, we become ensnared in a negative pattern that drives us to actions that, although possibly justifiable in biblical times, have ethically and politically unacceptable and even catastrophic consequences when repeated today.

A variety of possibilities exist for transforming perverted archetypes. For example, an ethnic group could make the political decision to opt out of the perverted pattern and work toward restoring the positive archetype. In the case of the Israeli-Palestinian conflict, both sides would have to develop a form of common government that would make it possible for Jews and Palestinians to live together in cooperation and tend the land of Israel/Palestine together.

Repeated failures in negotiated attempts to find such a solution have shown that peace is almost unthinkable unless both sides work to transform perverted archetypes as a prerequisite to peace negotiations. Since public authorities or political parties can hardly be expected to become active in this way, the success of this preliminary phase depends almost entirely on committed volunteers to transform the perverted archetypes.

During my last workshop in Jerusalem, together with the participants we developed and tried out, in the form of the group ritual described below, one possible form of healing work to transform these archetypes. Another ritual that can be performed in the context of private meditation is presented in the seven meditations found at the end of this half of the book.

Group Ritual

- The members of the group form a circle and concentrate first on personal grounding and sensing their inner connections to each other.
- One person from the group briefly describes the character of the perverted archetype to be transformed.
- By remembering relevant images, experiences, memories, etc., the group begins to manifest the essence of the alienated archetype outside the circle, behind their backs.
- When the pressure of the alienated forces become almost too strong to withstand, the sign is given to admit them into the center of the circle, where they are enclosed in a sphere of light.
- Then Sister Earth is asked to erect a column of violet light rising from the center. Violet is the color of transformation. The contents of the sphere rotate around this column and bathe in its light.
- Now the group makes its contribution to the transformation. Each participant sends a broad ray of love and compassion from his or her heart space into the center of the sphere. The help of the angels of transformation is summoned from cosmic space.
- When the process of transformation is complete, the group begins to sing in harmony so that the impulse of the transformed and purified archetype can spread throughout the land.
- The ritual is concluded by giving thanks.

Hopes for the Continuation of Earth's Evolution

According to observations I have compiled systematically for several years, the Earth's etheric space is currently involved in a profound transformation. This may sound surprising, because almost nothing of this transformation is outwardly visible. It is taking place in the subtle layers of earthly space.

In February 1998 I perceived the first sign that new foundations are being created for reality as we know it. Within the next three months, the spectrum of emanations from the land changed significantly. Air replaced Earth as the dominant element. In other words, our etheric space is no longer governed by the dense vibrations of matter but by the much subtler, more penetrable quality of consciousness.

It is almost impossible to describe all the events and fundamental changes in the Earth's space in the years that followed. Even now, a new wave of changes is set off every few months. The proportion of cosmic to earthly factors in the shaping of space has been reversed, and the roles of animals and elemental beings in the Earth's life-body are changing. We no longer live in a linearly imagined space but are confronted with a reality in which time and eternity—that is, different dimensions of being—will exist simultaneously in the same space.*

We can imagine the Earth's transformations as attempts at self-healing. In its millions of years of evolution, the Earth has learned to overcome all possible obstacles. Even the pitfall of ecological destruction may be simply one more hurdle for the Earth. From our personal experiences, we know that obstacles, instead of simply being disruptive, may also present welcome opportunities for new learning. Perhaps the Earth's consciousness also "learns" by confronting problems on the planet's surface. This may be why the Earth has decided to initiate complex transformations of its space rather than simply eliminating the obstacles through natural catastrophes.

But what do we mean by "transformations of space"? Obviously, the Earth is not a purely physical planet. It is surrounded by biological, energetic, and emotional spheres that make possible the many different developments on its surface. This is how the Earth's etheric space develops. In the evolutionary epoch now drawing to a close, the near-material etheric components of the fabric of space play a leading role. This is exactly the extension of the fabric of space that is most affected by ecological destruction. It is collapsing, but it is simultaneously being replaced by a new, multidimensional structuring of space.

In practical terms, this means that in spite of the intense, even fateful changes taking place in the invisible energetic and emotional layers of space, life on Earth is proceeding on its normal course. As I see it, a new Earth-space has already developed on these levels to a considerable extent. As soon as it becomes viable, the old etheric space will begin to be shed. This transformation of space is best compared to the shedding of a snake's skin. The old skin has become too tight and is already tattered in spots. No problem! Beneath it, a new, looser skin is developing, which will allow the snake to continue to grow. As soon as the new garment is ready, the old one will be cast off and the snake will be able to enjoy its new skin.

---

* In this context, see my three most recent books, *Turned Upside Down* (Lindisfarne); *Earth Changes, Human Destiny* and *The Daughter of Gaia* (both Findhorn Press).

When preparing for part of the Earth-healing seminar that I held in the spring of 2002, I discovered an "island of light" on the summit of a forgotten hill near Kiryat Tivon. By "islands of light," I mean the rounded energy fields that are appearing here and there in the landscape now that the transformation of the Earth has begun. These islands have the character of autonomous etheric spaces whose prevailing forces and qualities are completely different from those in the surrounding landscape. Surely they are examples of the multidimensional space of the future, present already in the form of islands of light. In this sense, light islands are the "seeds" of the Earth-space that will manifest in the future when all of the transformations have been successfully concluded. These islands, which are scattered all over the globe, confirm that the future already exists within the present. We can see them as guarantees that the Earth's transformation cannot fail, since it has already been successfully completed in spots.

As I stood in the light island of Kiryat Tivon, I was struck by the sensation that it actually belonged to Jerusalem, and safeguarded the future of that unfortunate city. But Jerusalem lies a hundred kilometers to the south! As it turns out, however, one of the four energy lines (ley lines) that give the Old City of Jerusalem its unique quality runs through the light island of Kiryat Tivon, thus obliterating the apparent distance between them.

Several days earlier, as I stood on the edge of the Jerusalem Forest, I tuned in to the inner quality of the hill where the Old City stands. I was drawn deep underground to the edge of a wonderful, light-filled space that pulsated within the hill. To identify its special quality, I asked it to manifest within my body, and I then felt the Tree of Life developing along my spine. According to the Revelation of John, the Tree of Life stands in the center of the "New Jerusalem"—a term that means nothing other than the transformed body of the Earth. The vision I received suggested that the quality characteristic of the newly forming Earth-cosmos is already anchored within the hill today. It is no coincidence, therefore, that the light island of Kiryat Tivon is knocking at the gates of Jerusalem. That is where the true place of peace is concealed.

Seven Meditations to Promote Peace in Ourselves and in Israel/Palestine

To enable anyone who chooses to do so to collaborate in working creatively toward peace in the Near East, I have developed a series of seven meditations that are intended to be practiced sequentially for seven successive days. If possible, they should be repeated several times a day, or the entire week of meditation can be repeated several times in a row.

It makes no difference at all where you are; you need not be traveling to the Near East. On the contrary, having participants scattered all over the globe will help disseminate the project as widely as possible.

- This project acts on the assumption that peace on Earth will not be found as long as we human beings have not learned to implant the blessed quality of peace in ourselves.
- As a second step, the impulse for peace is to be transferred to the countries of the Near East. This step is possible only as a result of resonance with the energy fields of Israel/Palestine, which is brought about by the meditant's inner images and feelings.
- We firmly believe that such an exercise can help to create conditions that will make peace possible in the Near East, even on the material level.

Some individual meditations are devoted to breaking down the main obstacles to peace, while others support specific energies that lead to peace.

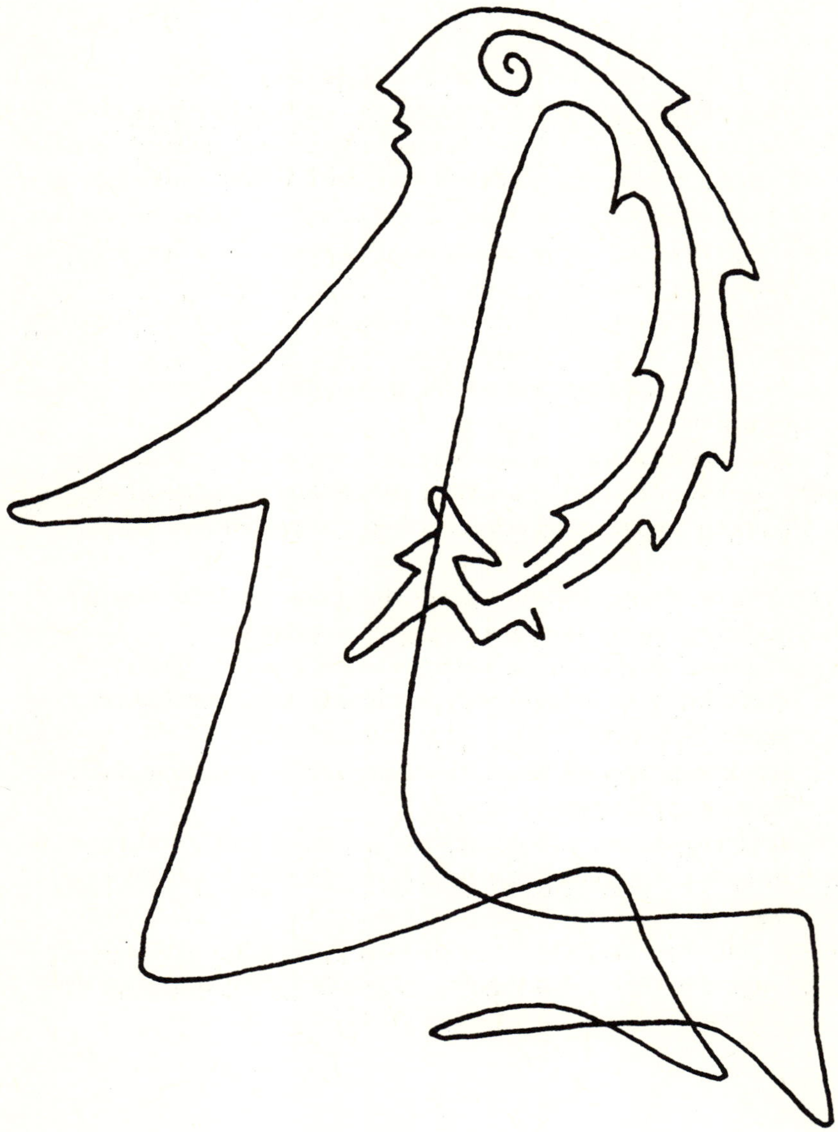

Sunday

Assignment of the Day: *To transmute the perversion of the female principle in ourselves and in the Near East.*

By now, suppression of the female principle in the Near East is so advanced that female forces have become instruments for patterns of violence. To name only one example, places vibrant with everyday life are transformed into places of death and juveniles are seduced into acting out masculine conflicts.

This meditation is intended to stimulate the return of the female principle to its true energy source.

Meditation for Sunday

- Find your place of inner stillness.
- Center yourself in the back of your head by finding the central point in the back of your head. From there, connect with cosmic dimensions.
- Next, beginning from the back of your head, construct an arching bridge behind you, running along your back.
- The far end of the bridge attaches to your sacrum. There you find a door. Go through the door, entering the rounded space of your abdomen.
- Standing in the middle of that inner space, send roots down deep into the Earth's core.
- Draw from there an impulse that is able to create a feeling of paradise there down between your hips.
- Allow the fragrance of paradise to ascend vertically, till it reaches your heart center.
- Immediately, your heart begins to pour out love-energy to all sides, and with it the message of the Holy Land.

Monday

Assignment for the Day: *To free yourself from the domination of the past.*

The second cause of the ongoing and repeated conflicts in the Near East has to do with a pattern of behavior that can best be described as the "absence of the present." Forced into a corset of beliefs centered on the conviction that the framework of reality is eternally fixed, individuals surrender to and become the victims of the consequences of their own mental patterns.

Through an encounter with our inner child, today's meditation leads us to identify with the present. The impulse of being rooted in the present should then be transferred to the Near East.

Meditation for Monday

- Sitting comfortably, fold your hands in your lap and spend a period of time in silence.
- Visualize your inner child standing on your folded hands. Support this image with your emotions.
- At the right moment, visualize your inner child pivoting upward until its feet are level with your third eye.
- Your inner child descends into your body through the door of your third eye until it stands on your pubic bone. As it lands, feel yourself united with the divine Now.
- Make sure that the quality that lights up in this moment spreads out in all directions. Imagine Jerusalem as its point of origin.

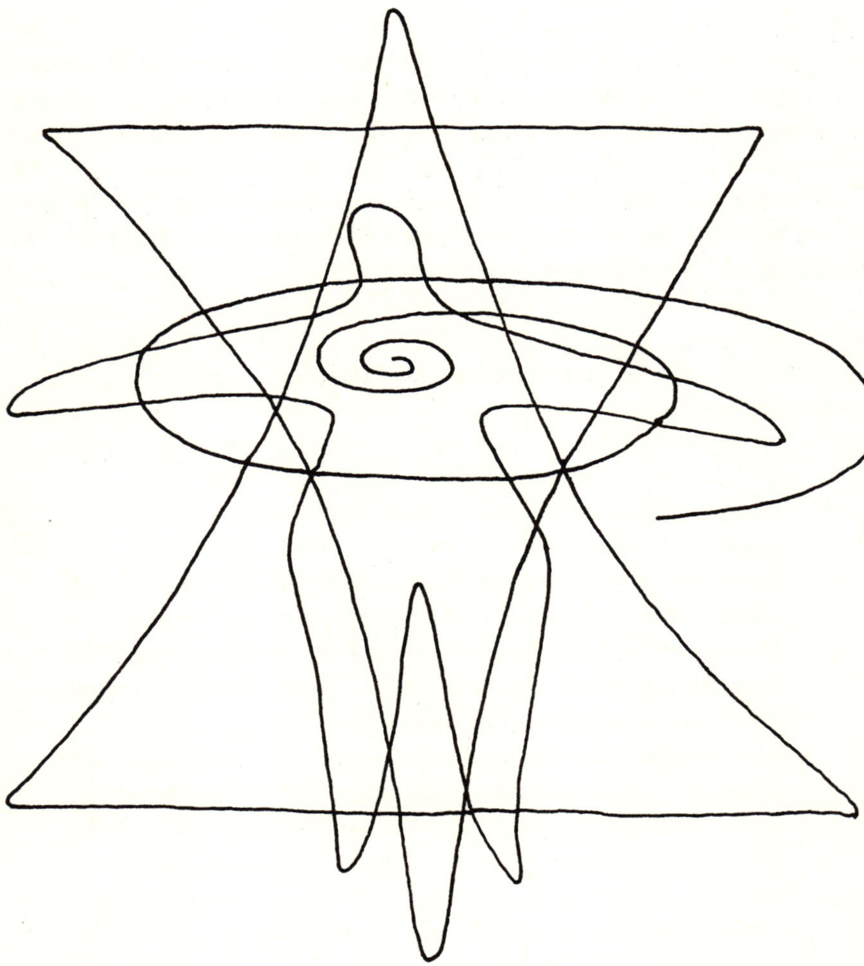

Tuesday

Assignment for the Day: *Fill the threatening emptiness between inhaling and exhaling with life-energy.*

The Holy Land is caught in a very dramatic situation, trapped in the empty space between inhaling and exhaling. On the one hand, the wonderful wave of revelation that provided humankind with new inspiration to reconnect with heaven and Earth is long since over. On the other hand, the Near East lacks the capacity to let this inspiration pour into society and between people and by doing so to breathe out. This capacity has long since been fragmented by rigidified religious ideas, military conflicts, and forced poverty.

The intent of this meditation is to remind the Holy Land of its original role within the Organism of the Earth. Through the heart zone of Israel/Palestine, the inspiration of the marriage between heaven and Earth should be exhaled into the horizontal network of life.

Meditation for Tuesday

- Unite with the bowl of the Earth below you and the dome of heaven above. Imagine earth-forces spiraling heavenward through you and heaven-forces moving through you in the form of a column of light that sinks deep into the Earth. Sense the interchange of these forces within yourself.
- Now imagine these energy flows being caught consciously by a crystal in the center of your heart. As a result, your heart-center begins to shine and radiate light. Its rays reach far into your surroundings, blessing the forces and beings of earthly space.
- Now link all the forces and beings of earthly space together with delicate threads of light, focusing the network in a point located behind your navel. Sense yourself in the center of a network that connects everything with everything else.
- Now transfer the center of the network from your navel to the landscape between the Dead Sea and the Sea of Galilee. From the geomantic perspective, this is the World Navel.
- Breathe for a while in harmony with the landscape of the place to strengthen the World Navel. When you breathe in, you draw the Earth's network of life together; when you breath out, love-energy pours out over all the world.

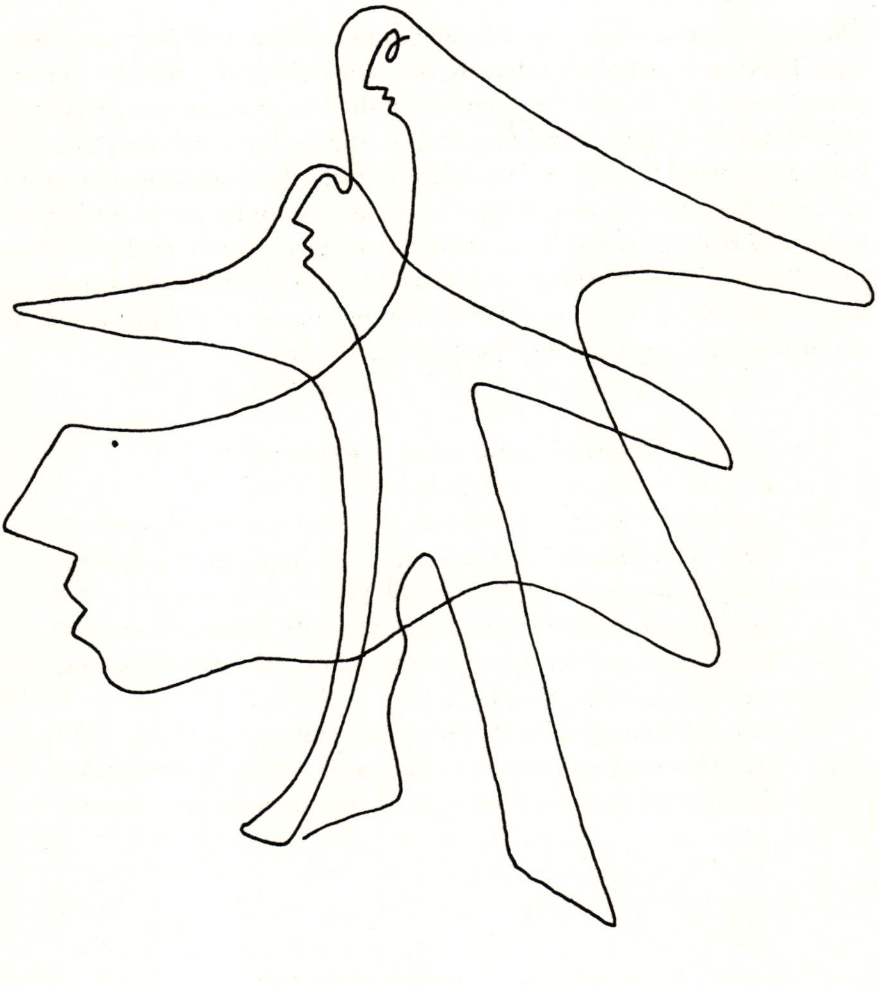

Wednesday

Assignment for the Day: *To invite the spiritual world to become active in the Near East.*

The term "spiritual world" describes the world of the dead living in the hereafter. They are human beings like us, but they belong to a different dimension of existence. We are talking only about those souls whose personal development is already sufficiently advanced to help the living in times of need. On the one hand, these souls have access to stores of universal knowledge; on the other, they are also rich in experiences of how things are in the human world and how the snares of personal development can be avoided. Their advice might help resolve current emergencies in Israel/Palestine, where the words or the help of the wise individuals who appeared as prophets throughout history has never been more needed than it is now.

Meditation for Wednesday

- Decide on a specific individuality familiar to you from the holy scriptures of the Jews, Christians, or Muslims. Ask this individuality to intervene helpfully in the Near East right now.
- In your back, sense the presence and qualities of this individuality.
- Guide these qualities through your body to the front and spread them out over the Near East.
- Extricate yourself carefully from the connection you have established between your chosen individuality and the Near East. Ask that this connection be maintained and strengthened.

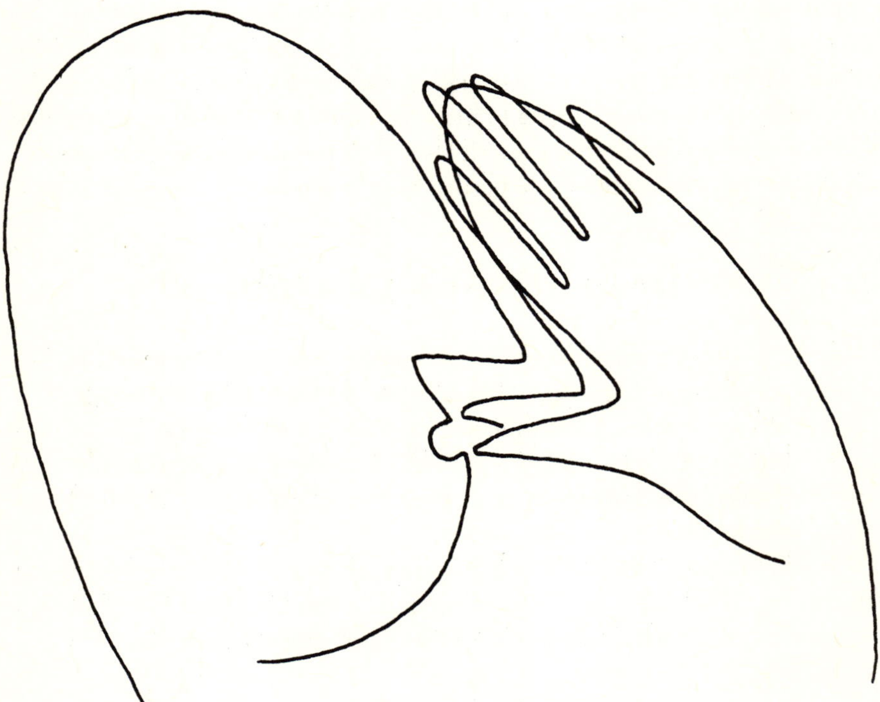

Thursday

Assignment for the Day: *To direct attention to loving connections and the dance of life.*

To introduce healing processes in the Near East, we should draw public attention to the country's living reality. Today, however, public attention is focused almost exclusively on the catastrophic political situation, which is subject to commentary in the media and broadcast throughout the world. Our gaze, held spellbound in the bloody knots of the conflict, must be released from this suicidal lethargy. The antidote to political rigidity, the force that will set us free, lies in the radiant presence of life, which corresponds to the love-energy dwelling in the essential core of the human being.

Meditation for Thursday

- Form a pyramid with your hands, with its tip at the level of your third eye.
- Your thumbs are right in front of your mouth, lightly touching your lips. Leave a small gap between your thumbs for your breath to flow through.
- With consciousness and sensitivity, breathe into the channel between your thumbs several times to enliven the pyramid with your breath.
- Next, inaudibly whisper a message to that aspect of life that is important to you in relationship to the Near East. You may want to address the souls of those driving the conflict in the Near East or whisper hope to one of its victims. Through the contact between your lips and the tips of your thumbs, the message becomes perceivable even for layers of existence that have no physical ears.
- In conclusion, lay your hands in your lap and immerse yourself in the space that becomes manifest through this communication.

Friday

Assignment for the Day: *To transform the dominance of rigid patterns of thought into a network of loving connections*

An important thread in the healing process in the Near East has to do with breaking down petrified ideas, thought patterns, and spiritual dogmas. These are specific archetypes or forces of feeling and thinking that have become perverted as the result of historical or religious developments at some point in the past. Trapped in their negative form, they are now entrenched but unnoticed in the souls of the ethnic groups involved in the conflict. They influence the shattered relationships among individuals and nations in the Near East and prevent a peaceful solution.

Since we are dealing here with divinely inspired archetypal patterns that were later perverted, their original quality can be restored at any time.

Meditation for Friday

- Feel yourself secure, well grounded, and embedded in silence within a rounded, protective sheath.
- To begin the transformation, choose one of the perverted archetypal patterns that sow death and destruction in the Near East.
- Through relevant images, experiences, or memories, allow the power (or impotence) of the alienated archetype to manifest behind you.
- At the same time, saturate your body's vibrations with love-energy originating in the center of your heart. This makes you able to transform the most vicious thoughts and feelings without harm to yourself.
- After the pressure of alienated energies behind you has abated, allow these energies to flow through your love-saturated body.
- Observe this process of transformation with an open heart. Create more heart energy in the center of your heart, as needed.
- Sense the energy of the transformed archetype as it has developed within your protective sheath. Allow it to flow or radiate out into the wide world, making sure that its blessings are concentrated in the Near East in particular.

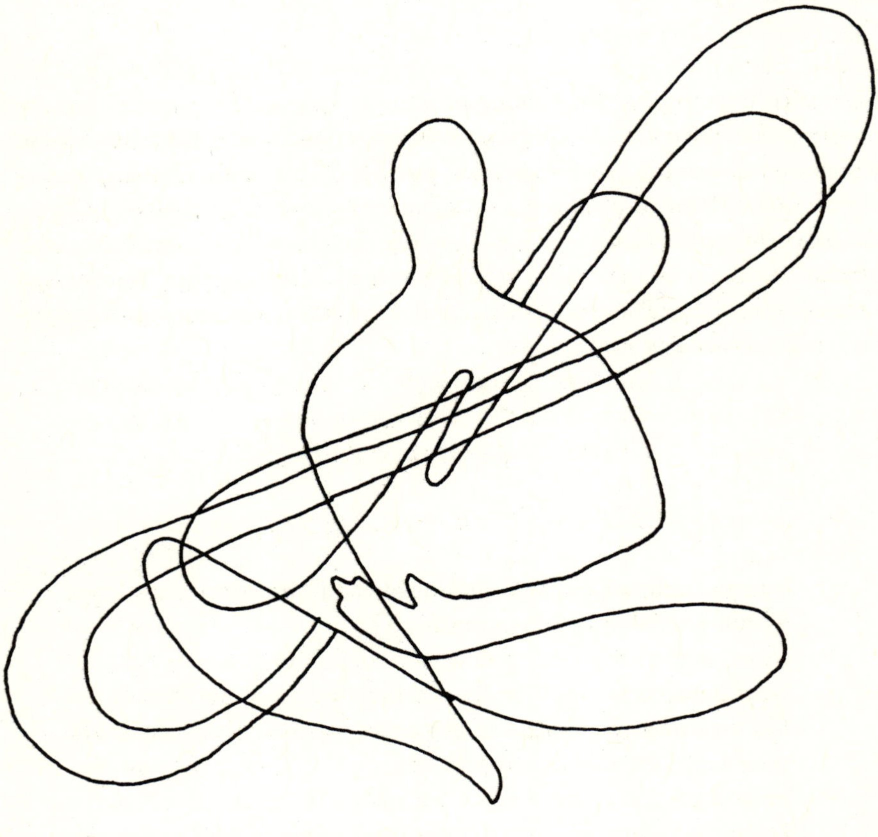

Saturday

Assignment for the Day: *To foster hope for the ongoing transformation of the Earth.*

Life on Earth only appears to be continuing on its accustomed course. This physically determined experience is illusory, because fateful changes are occurring on the invisible energetic and emotional levels of earthly space, which we humans can barely perceive. As a result of intensive inner transformations in recent years, a new living, energetic level of space is being built up for the planet. When this layer is fully viable, the old one will begin to be cast off. Before we are caught up in its dissolution, we human beings must learn to tune in to the new layer, to participate in its abundant life, and to experience its all-pervading peace.

Meditation for Saturday

- Sit in silence for a while, concentrating on the center of your heart.
- Imagine yourself going as far out into the space in front of you as you possibly can. Then return in an arc to the center of your heart. Repeat this several times.
- Next, imagine yourself going as far as you possibly can into the space behind your back. Return again in an arc to the center of your heart. Repeat this several times.
- Now push the space behind you forward, in the direction of embodied life. Push the space in front of your chest backward, in the direction of eternity.
- Meanwhile, pay attention to the energy or quality being engendered in the center of your heart. Hold on to it for a while, then let it radiate out into a world that longs for healing and peace. Do not forget Israel/Palestine, the legendary World Navel.
- Imagine yourself standing in the center of the Holy Land. From there, your love radiates outward in circular waves that bestow blessings on the Earth's entire energy field and all the beings immersed in it.

Cosmograms to Support Places of Healing in the Near East

In the process of putting this book together, I devised cosmograms to support the self-healing and reopening of some of the important energy-centers of the Near East. Cosmograms are complex characters that directly convey information on multiple levels at once, together with the related energy structures. The process of developing a cosmogram imbues it with enough carrying power of its own so that it does not need to be understood rationally for its effects to unfold. It does, however, require conscious attention.* One possible way of allowing the cosmograms to work is to photocopy them, cut them out, and post them at various places in your personal surroundings where they can be perceived readily. In this case, their effects would be activated by paying attention to them on a daily basis.

A second option is to recreate them in other artistic media. Painting, dance, performance, etc. are all possible. The only important thing is to make sure that the original message is not lost. To prevent that, I have included a text explaining the message of each cosmogram in terms accessible to consciousness.

All of the cosmograms have been devised to support and promote not only places of healing in the Near East but also the corresponding aspects of the human individual.

---

* For the theory of cosmograms as a form of universal language, consult my books *Healing the Heart of the Earth* and *Earth Changes, Human Destiny* (both Findhorn Press).

Cosmogram dedicated to the cosmic aspect of the heart-center

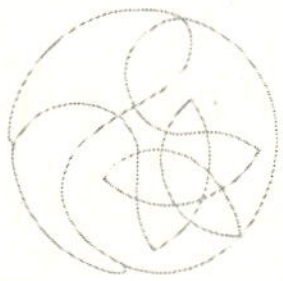

Related to the individual human being, this cosmogram helps the cosmic expanses of the heart unfold. At the same time, it supports one of the Near East's most important heart-centers, located in the chest of the Sphinx at Giza. Connections to various extensions of the universe that transcend space and time are anchored in the Giza plateau with its Pyramids and Sphinx. Similarly, individuals can connect with eternity's primal space through the cosmic aspect of the heart-center. The corresponding aspect of the human heart chakra is located at the rear of the heart-center.

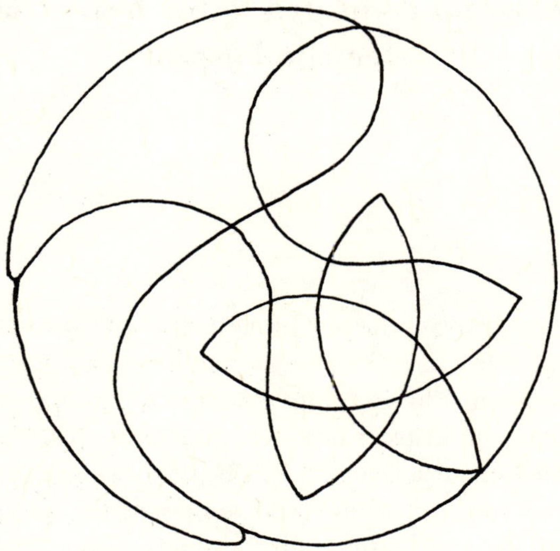

Cosmogram dedicated to the heart chakra's elemental aspect

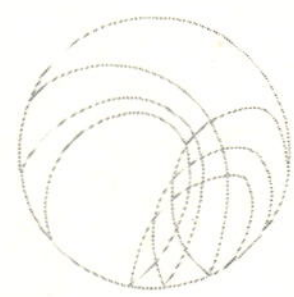

This cosmogram involves the part of nature's heart that is embedded in the wholeness of our own heart, since we human beings are also part of the natural world. Like all other living beings, we also share in the beating of nature's heart. This cosmogram helps us unite with the roots of the heart-energy that is deeply anchored in our sexuality. There exists the source of primeval power that can empower love to become creative in daily life. On the cosmogram there is depicted the door leading into the depths of the Earth, which opens to the right. This cosmogram also supports the opening of the heart-center of St. Catherine's Monastery at the foot of Mount Sinai, which plays a similar role in the landscape of the Near East.

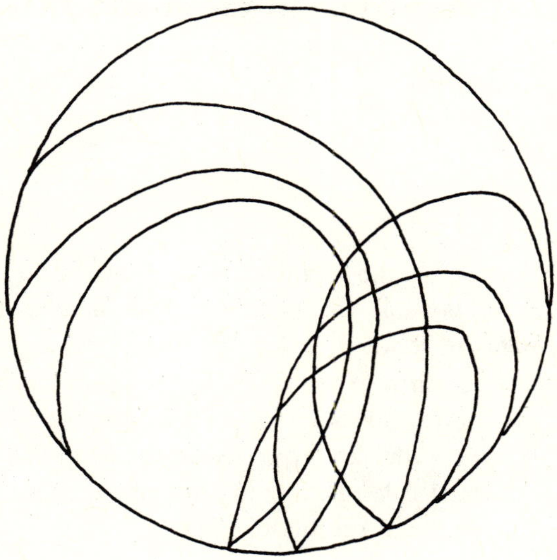

Cosmogram of life abundant

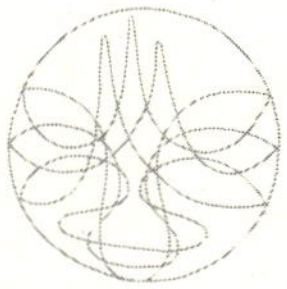

This cosmogram shows the joyful expression of the four elements that interweave to make possible the paradisiacal abundance of the manifest world. The elements of Water and Air (left and right) are balanced out by Fire (yang) above and Earth (Yin) below. In the human being, this cosmogram relates to the conduction of sexual energies into the forms and connections of daily life, where they are expressed in the form of creative cooperation. In the case of Israel/Palestine, the impulse of abundant life is embodied by the landscape around Elat on the Red Sea.

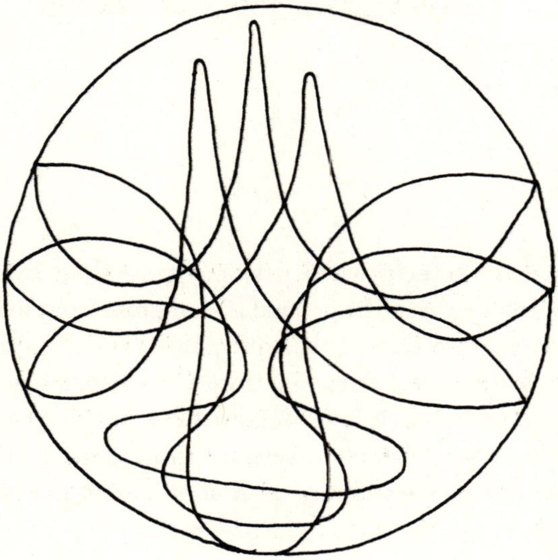

Cosmogram for grounding

This cosmogram can help when personal grounding is inadequate. It is important to emphasize that the general loss of grounding in places and individuals is due to something more than alienation from the being of the Earth. We should also learn to free ourselves from the illusory space of the present age and to take root in the self-renewing earthly cosmos. This cosmogram has been created not only to stimulate personal grounding in the newly emerging etheric space but also to support renewal of the planet's grounding chakra at the Dead Sea.

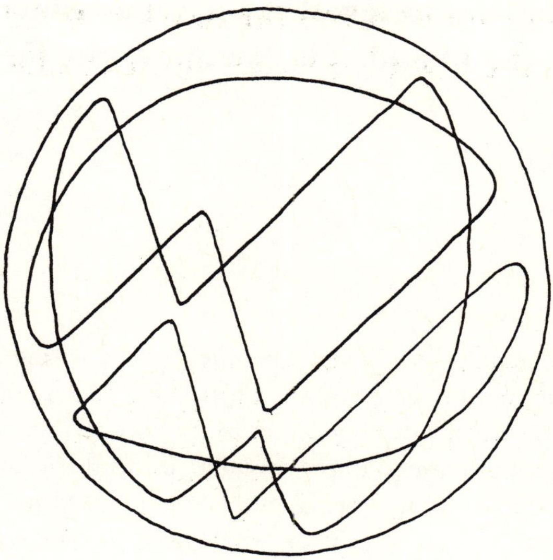

Cosmogram to reveal the navel of Israel/Palestine on the Masada plateau above the Dead Sea

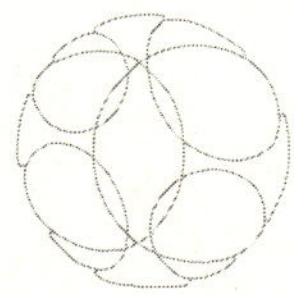

Because Masada is known almost entirely as the setting of a collective suicide, it is important to emphasize the plateau's role as a holy site, the *omphalos* (Gr. "world navel") or holy center of the country, the "golden sphere" in which everything is united to preserve and affirm the source of being. In the landscape as in the human being, the navel is related to centering and balancing the entire organism on the vital-energetic, emotional, and spiritual planes.

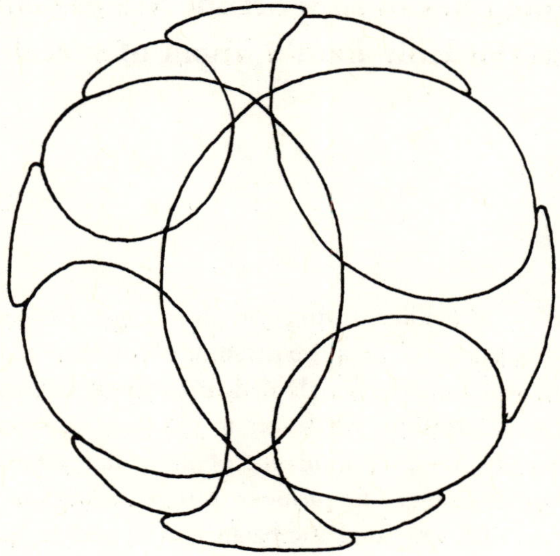

Cosmogram to support the Sea of Galilee as the Holy Land's organ of speech

To allow the Sea of Galilee to function as an organ of speech, the influx and outflow of the Jordan take on the rhythms of inhaling and exhaling. The river's two banks represent the female-male polarity. The West Bank (on the left in the figure) contributes yin forces to the creative interplay, the East Bank yang forces, in a way reminiscent of the creative role of the larynx chakra in the human being. The purpose of this cosmogram is to reenliven Israel/Palestine's ability to restore the balance of opposites and to allow the resulting peace to resound throughout the world.

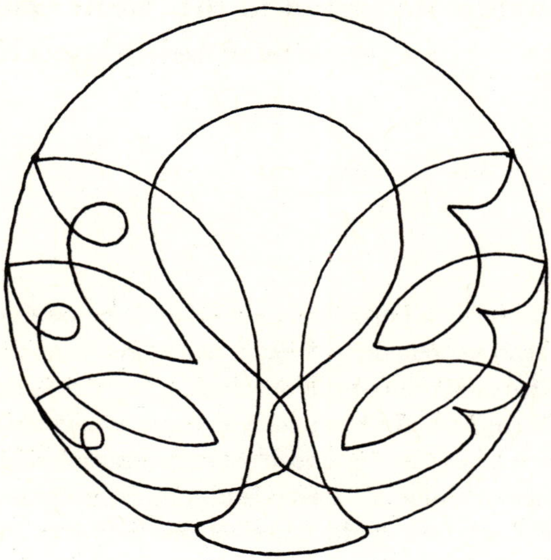

Cosmogram dedicated to the "heart channel" in the human being

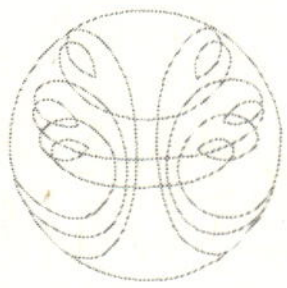

The heart channel is a horizontal channel of light connecting the three aspects of the heart-center: the cosmic aspect at the rear, the center of the heart, and the chakra at the front of the chest, which pours out heart energy. This cosmogram supports the heart channel's consecrated task of concentrating and pouring out heart energy and activates Jerusalem's heart-center, located within the rock of Golgotha. This complex heart-center is associated with the Tree of Life that stands in the center of the "new Jerusalem," the transformed, peace-pervaded earthly cosmos. The form of the Tree of Life is evident on the cosmogram.

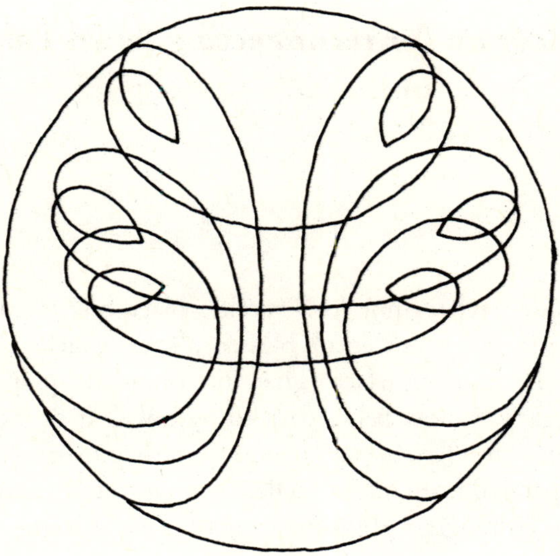

Cosmogram for reconnecting Israel/Palestine

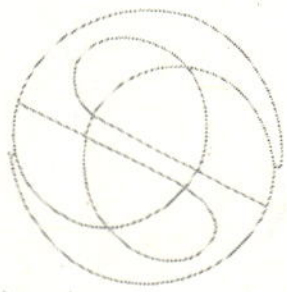

This cosmogram relates not to a specific place but to the country as a whole. In the context of our entire blessed planet, Israel/Palestine is only a tiny point on the Earth's surface. That this rounded up space, one of the Earth's vital organs, is now being divided by a wall is an expression of the inner separation of modern human beings from their own wholeness. Within us, female is separated from male, intellect from intuition, and the heart from the whole. This cosmogram sings the song of reconnection.

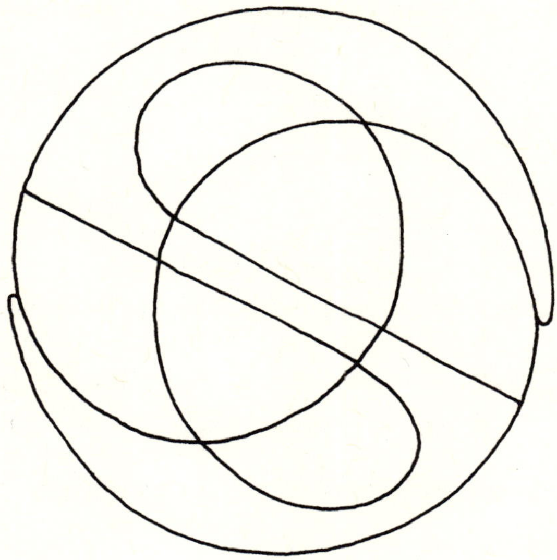

Crossing the Threshold

You have arrived at an important threshold. After travelling through the book to this point, the region of conscious reasoning and resulting intuitive action is now behind you. Before you an entirely different area is vibrating. If you do not prepare yourself for it in the right way, you may be disappointed. If you enter with misconceptions or false expectations, the space you are about to enter may not open itself to you. Its treasures will then remain hidden from you.

The composition of this book in two parts corresponds to the usual articulation of sacred space. Crossing the threshold, you leave behind the vestibule to enter the sanctuary itself. The first part of the book is based on different layers of human consciousness; the second part is written in such a way that the divine presence—called by its author "Christ consciousness"—expresses itself directly. Do not miss meeting it!

My advice is to enter the text where your intuition leads you. Read here and there. Let yourself be freely guided through the text. Allow the text to touch you in its own way. It has its own intelligence and knows what it wants to tell you personally. Listen to it on all levels.

Divinity does not need a multitude of words to tell what it wants you to know. In any given moment, you will feel what is important for you. It might be enough to read just a few passages to begin with. Then, later, read other passages.

It is important that the text incarnate in you, that every cell absorb it. In this way, the text will become grounded and you will make it possible that it becomes creative in the world.

Good luck for your continuation of the journey!

Part II

Ana Pogačnik

Reconciling the Old and the New

Messages of Heart's Love, Messages of Christ's Power

How it all happened

When the publisher asked me to write a section of this book, I had no idea what themes, messages, or texts might come to me. So when I first began to write, I was completely open and free of preconceived ideas.

Each message that was then revealed through this openness to me was a true gift that I received gladly. So I decided to publish all of them, not merely a selection.

Although I already had quite a bit of experience in translating messages from other "worlds," other dimensions, or other levels of existence, receiving and transcribing these messages was a new experience and a new challenge for me.

The incredible power, energy and indescribable love that flowed alongside and through the messages were *so* strong that they became sometimes almost unbearable and always moved me deeply in my heart as I wrote.

I see these messages more as a glimpse into life's mysteries than as a textbook for life or any sort of "instruction" in how we ought to live. They encourage us to look into life's depths honestly—without masks, fear, or barriers; with joy and zest for life.

I do not experience the messages as a critique of beliefs or believers, for they repeatedly emphasize the freedom of heart and of decisions. The only thing that may have been subject to more critical scrutiny is the rigidity of the religions and churches that base themselves on the original beliefs. This too, however, is not intended as criticism but simply as a glimpse behind the scenes.

As a whole, the text resounds in me as an appeal to us humans to finally decide in favor of our own inner truth, to open ourselves to pure love and heart strength, and to free ourselves of all possible projections, restrictive rules, and seductive untruths.

I am especially glad for the opportunity to publish these messages about the *heart's power* at this particular moment. In my perception, the power of the heart is again coming to the fore in the present time. For more than a year I have been noticing a change in the layers and in that way also a stronger presence of the power of the heart, part of which is also the power of the Christ. This change is readily perceptible and tangible, both in human beings and in all parts of the natural world, and it is becoming increasingly concretely anchored in the landscape.

Thus I see the entire process of the Earth's current transformation as a phase of balance—or better to say of the transition to equilibrium—in which everything is being balanced out and connected in the center, in the heart, so that it may act—and above all, BE—together and in one with everything that is.

Oberweningen, January 30, 2004

Messages along the way

We immerse ourselves in inner stillness and allow ourselves to be touched by profound peace. For a brief moment, we let go of everything, freeing our souls and hearts. In this serenity, we sink deep into the power of the heart, allowing it to permeate and overflow us until we become one with it.

We open ourselves to the heart's expansiveness and allow ourselves to transcend our own limitations for a moment. And exactly in this brief moment, we can experience what it means to be part of the whole and completely abandoned to eternity. All that counts is love, is the power of the heart.

In such moments of absolute absorption, there is no longer any "Why" or any "How," nor is there any doubt or fear. In this state, deeply touched and overwhelmed by eternity, we can simply only BE.

The messages before us here are an attempt to grasp in words this pure, profound heart's power in words. In this way they are a translation of this energy flow, which is involved in a constant and eternal process of development. The messages serve as a vessel for this flowing power.

The power that has been ever present in us for eons and lives alongside us.
The power we have drawn from for a long time.
The power that needs no objective source because it is itself the source.
The power that can touch the depths of the heart and can lead and accompany us into the depths of our own hearts.
The power that bears within it the entire creation of life.
The power that was through religions shaped into rigid form.
The power that gives the impulse of life a possibility to express itself.
The power onto which we put great hopes in every moment, and in which there are constantly made many projections.
The power that opens the heart and needs openness of the heart to be able to work through life.
This is the heart's power and in that way a part of what we call the power of the Christ.

The messages are not a text that one can read like any other, but a flow that we should let run through us as we read. They are also not a text that can be skimmed quickly, but one that needs depth, and to be understood with the heart and not with the head. So it is not possible to read these messages as a book. We can only allow them to sink part by part, step by step gradually into us.

It is a gift that was given me, and so I ask you to accept it as a gift, too.

Please, let's put aside all potential thoughts, our own projections, unnecessary judgments, glorification, possible criticisms and exaggerated enthusiasm and allow the power to flow through the messages, to touch us and in that way to speak to us.

We should become an empty vessel, ready to receive.

Oberweningen, January 28, 2004

The Messages

Purity of soul is the key to resurrection—and not the reverse, i.e., that the resurrection is the key to purity of soul.

This is one of the greatest "errors" in the history of religions. There is no soul that does not carry the most profound purity in itself. There is no individual who does not carry this seed of truth in his or her own self, own heart. The key is exactly this profound truth, which connects us all in oneness.

What Jesus wanted to give us with his life as an example is not a miracle story. It is a story, not of a distant event meant to awaken awe in us, but of the truth of our own hearts. Each one of us lives Jesus within. Each of us has the opportunity to bring Jesus' experiences to light. It is no mystery, and again, it is no miracle. It was, and still is, a reality that can touch us at any moment if we are truly ready to allow it to approach and are really ready to be touched.

The moment of deepest truth and cognition will come when we finally allow this reality to awaken within us and waken us to life.

When this happens, we will also be ready to see ourselves as miracles, and only then will we accept ourselves as miracles of life.

We will no longer need to project miracles onto something outside ourselves or look for stories we could describe as miraculous. We will need a sense of wonder only until the moment when we will be ready to recognize ourselves as wondrous. Then we will really be able to see life as life and ourselves as a mirror of life.

Jesus lived all this as an example, to show us that we are free to take life and live it as our heart shows and tells us. There are no boundaries and also no limitations. We are the only limit that exists.

We are always looking for an end to eternity. Even when we realize that eternity cannot be bounded, we are still not ready to accept life's infinite freedom, to finally start to live it.

Oberweningen, January 30, 2004

By considering Jesus' life and his activities as a miracle, we limit ourselves. We deprive ourselves of the possibility of experiencing and living these truths for ourselves.

We project it all onto Jesus as a personality and forget that we ourselves also embody exactly the strength that Jesus lived. At every moment, we have the opportunity to allow this power to come to life within us.

Jesus gave life the gift of his purity of heart. That's why he was able to live what he did, to give the gift of true purity to himself, others, and all of humankind. He was living the source of his own heart and thus could experience himself as a real part of life. He did not need to fear life because he was not afraid of himself.

The story of Jesus' life is meant to serve as an example to us and not to awaken awe in us. In viewing it with awe, we close ourselves off from life's energy. We distort the message that Jesus wanted to give us on our way. This runs as follows: to live the deepest purity of heart, and not to fear the deepest purity of heart.

We deprive ourselves of the heart's life power and this path in life by projecting them onto the figure of Jesus. We think, "Yes, that was how Jesus lived." Yes, Jesus really lived this way, but this does not mean that we also cannot, may not, or should not live this way. He lived his life as an example, to show us the way and not to confine us through our own awe.

By placing Jesus on a pedestal, we created a separation within ourselves. We have concentrated on the outer energy and figure of Jesus instead of on our own heart's power. In this way we relinquished responsibility for ourselves.

This is the point where the search for inner strength and the longing for the heart's eternal love begin.

We projected them so strongly onto the figure of Jesus, even transforming them into cumbersome religions, that we forget that the way leads inward, not outward.

In this way we closed the door on ourselves.

There exists no power that could flow from outside to show us the way of our heart's light. There is no light that could shine into us from outside to illuminate the purity of our heart's power. There is no spark that could spring from outside to ignite true love in us. No truth from outside can awaken our inner truth. We can really reach ourselves only from within. Only through ourselves we can bestow the spark of life and purity of heart on love and life.

Oberweningen, May 11, 2003

Jesus had the courage to live the power of the heart and to bring it into life. He also had the courage to take this step far in advance and to blaze the first trail for us all. Thus he transmitted purest heart-quality into life and anchored it. He made it so distinct that it gained a form and the power to manifest—which still does not mean that it is limited to working through one person only. It needed this initial clear, pure embodiment to anchor itself in the Earth and in humankind, but should not stay limited because of that.

This is the power that is called the power of Christ.
This is the deepest and purest power of the heart.
This is the power that can be called unconditional and boundless heart's love in the purest sense.

This is an *eternal* power, which clearly tells us that it could not come into being or develop through Jesus Christ.

His task was to bring this divine energy into life in such a direct, tangible form that it could become anchored in matter. Through him it was able to become real and truly active, clear and penetrating, for the first time. This was not only the first impulse but at the same time the foundation.

Unfortunately, after all this time and after many misinterpretations, we have forgotten what the true meaning of Jesus' life was and still is.

Through the construction of the religions the enormous impulse lost a great deal of its power. The living portion of this energy petrified and died, not with Jesus' death, as we so often believe, but with the rigidity and hardness of the religions.

We have allowed this strength to lie in each of us, passive, buried, forgotten and petrified. Each of us has allowed the power of the Christ to die within us.

As humankind, we even used this purest heart's power to gain predominance and authority through restrictive religions.

It is this predominance and authority that destroy the living portion of the heart-energy and life-energy, limiting our freedom of the heart.

Only parts through which it was possible to develop a miraculous story were consciously selected from Jesus' life and death, to engender fear of the divine, to hold the reins of human beings and to control life.

The greatness and the divinity of Jesus were and still are misused to show us our smallness and to confine us within rigid frames and limits.

Jesus was consciously exalted as the Chosen One to ultimately eliminate the danger that we would dare to develop same greatness and grow into this infinite divine love.

Divine love became instead of a power a burden.

The purity of heart that was exemplified and brought so close to us through Jesus' presence was limited again.

In this way it was not only weakened but also tailored to exactly defined ideas and rules. We have forced infinite divine love into a mold, so that what was once alive is now merely a stencil.

But it is the living part of the heart's power that Jesus exemplified so authentically with his life:

Divine love is love that originates in freedom of heart.
Infinite power of the heart is the power of life.

We can bring this energy effectively into life only if we are ready and willing to live it.

Words are one thing, no matter how beautiful, but living them is something else entirely.

The same is true of divine love, which has always existed but was able to anchor itself in matter again only through the presence of Jesus.

Oberweningen, May 11, 2003

Profound, divine power of the heart has been present since the beginning of life, but not with the intensity and quantity that became possible through Jesus' embodiment.

To help us understand this thought, let's briefly consider the process of humankind's development.

When we human beings were still deeply involved in the process of becoming individual, independent beings, we were not yet aware of any separation from the whole or oneness. In prehistoric times, humankind was really still part of the whole. There were no boundaries and limitations. We were not separated from the divine presence and universal divinity yet.

The feeling of what was outside and what was inside had not yet developed properly because everything was one.

When we chose the path of personal individualization, we also automatically fell into the process of gradual limiting. This was necessary and inevitable in our process of development, for without those limits we would not have been able to follow the path of the independent individual. Only in this way could we develop a sense of our own personal entirety and unity.

Because we followed the path of individualization, we began more and more to separate inside from outside.

As a consequence of this process, we also developed a different connection to the divine. Instead of being an inherent part of us, it became something that flowed in and alongside us.

This is why we needed the new impulse that was embodied so strongly through Jesus. We needed to anchor the divine in us to establish a new connection to the heart's power within us.

Prior to this time, the connection was too weak for us to sense the divine or carry it within us, let alone live it, in the world of personal individuality and the world of duality.

We can identify Jesus' incarnation as a new and deeper anchor of the divine love in humankind, and an important step in humankind's development: one that made it possible for us to go one level deeper in our union with the divine.

The connection between outside and inside was again made present and alive.

This was a new union with the whole.

But if we continue to trace our development, we will also realize that when the union occurred, we were not ready to enter into the connection effectively or maintain it with sufficient intensity.

We were still too involved in separation and delineation to hold the connecting bridge. We started to look up to Jesus because he was able to be such a link with his soul and his body. He was living this connection that otherwise remained more of a longing than a reality.

This is where the outward projection of the divine began. The anchoring of divine love through Jesus could no longer be seen as an embodiment of the divine power. It became a personification that was clearly defined and maintained by remaining fixed on a single person.

At this point, we began to set limits on the infinite. We became even more heavily invested in the process of duality that had developed out of the separation of inside and outside.

We excluded ourselves from connecting with the divine in order to project divinity onto Jesus. The result of this projection is Jesus as God.

We no longer realized that each of us bears the divine within and that Jesus represented only the initial impulse to focus this connection and thus to intensify and enable it.

We chose a long route for ourselves. With time, the path that led us to this exaggerated outward orientation and projection on all levels has only grown stronger. Matter and materialism have become increasingly important, and even the divine and the heart's most profound love-power have been projected entirely outward.

Oberweningen, May 12, 2003

The religions that developed on the basis of pure heart's power have even supported our outward-directed orientation.

A great power was born through the religions, a force that could dominate and control us.

To maintain and implement this force, it was necessary that our attention be focused outside of ourselves. The separation between inside and outside thus came at exactly the right time. The disconnect and division was used to make us forget and even deny our sense of our own selves, our strength and heart's love. As a result, the religions were able to maintain control over us.

Jesus' lifetime represents a very decisive moment when many opportunities and many possible directions were present simultaneously. It was a time that contributed very strong impulses to the process of evolution, regardless of which direction we as humankind would ultimately choose. For a while, everything hung in the balance, but the situation was misused to assume power.

Of course, that was and is the only right path for us to take. There could have been no better opportunity to experience and sense the divide between ourselves and the divine.

It was a good way for us to learn to live as individuals, although we first lost this possibility for quite a long time. Actually, we abandoned it as we prepared out of deepest religious beliefs to renounce our inner freedom.

We were ready to allow the profound longing for connection always so vigorously present in our core to go up in smoke.

Our sense of security, our confidence in externalized power and an externalized God, was strong enough to suppress our inner strength and inner energy.

We set our hopes on external help instead of developing inner potentials.

Instead of activating divine energy within ourselves, we directed our prayers toward an externalized God.

Instead of allowing the power of the Christ to awaken within us and become anchored in us, we projected it onto the figure of Jesus. In this process, we forgot who we really are.

As humankind, we were so blinded by external power and faith that we were even willing, in the name of purest heart's love, to destroy others who did not believe in our external God and to deny them the right to life.

Not only did we bury our own freedom of heart, we also went so far as to believe that everyone had to do the same in the name of Divine Love, out of respect for Divine Love. Drastically simplified, we can say that boundless heart's love became the reason and the weapon for the bloody Crusades. This may be difficult to believe and accept, but unfortunately it is true.

In the beginning was Jesus, who embodied the purest love of divine power of the heart. True love, true light, and true energy stood behind his deeds. He was led by the power of the heart. But what became of it? In all the religious wars, whether in the past or still raging around the world, where was and is this pure love, this light, and this power of the heart? Where was and is the Christ-power in us? Where is the infinite freedom of love within us, if we are still ready to accept the chains of rigid religious dogmas? Where is true love in all this? Where is our heart's love for ourselves?

Obenweningen, May 12, 2003

It took us a very long time to finally notice that we need freedom of heart if we are to serve life and, through it, ourselves. We searched outside of ourselves for the divine for a long time before we finally realized that we had lost ourselves.

In relinquishing our inner freedom, we have distorted Jesus' message. Instead of living the reality of the heart's freedom, we caged the power of love. In our desire to do right according to rules and dogmas, we were ready to bury our own deepest longing for freedom of heart.

In this blinded faith, we even accepted the idea of sin, which destroyed the last seed of freedom of heart and life.

Hoping to gain dignity and experience enlightenment, we gave our power into the hands of others and thought ourselves small and unworthy.

We were willing to play this somewhat degrading game with ourselves until we came so far that we were finally ready to recognize the truth of love, of the heart, of the divine, and to rediscover the desire for inner truth. Through these we had the strength to open our eyes again, and we gave our deep longing to be one with everything the freedom and opportunity to unfold. As long as we were not ready to see the divine in ourselves, the connection between inside and outside was not possible. The unity of life cannot be experienced through separation and duality. Connection to what is outside ourselves can arise only out of deepest inner connectedness.

We shut ourselves off from the divine because we were no longer able to draw on our own inner strength.

We sought strength in an external God; we projected divine energy onto spiritual teachers and gurus, forgetting that this energy is inherent in us and that we are the ones to bring it to life.

Through the renewed search for heart's love in ourselves, we have reactivated the strength that led us back to the path of freedom and connection.

At this point the time has come for us to receive the real messages that Jesus exemplified and prepared for us, without perverting, misunderstanding, or misusing them in any way.

It's as if a great circle has had to go through one complete rotation to arrive, under totally different circumstances and with totally different heart-knowledge, at the point where openness and freedom became strong enough to actualize and live divine heart's love. Above all, this is the point where we recognize our readiness and desire to connect in a new way with all that exists, to be a part of the whole and through this to espouse the divine once again.

This does not mean stepping back into times when we as humankind experienced and lived in duality, in separation. Instead, it means using the energy of personal individuality, which we developed through separation, to open ourselves to being part of the ocean of the heart's eternal love.

Oberweningen, May 13, 2003

It makes no sense to give us suggestions if we are not ready to receive them. Instructions have no value if we do not want to receive and open ourselves for them. We should not only open ourselves to hear teachings but also be ready to understand them with our deepest being, with our hearts.

The doors remain barred as long as we do not long for heart-knowledge.

And until this longing is transformed into desire for inner truth, we cannot appreciate the value of such suggestions.

Jesus' life clearly revealed this. We had not yet progressed far enough, our longing for profound truth was not mature enough to understand his messages, so we garbled and falsified them in ways that almost make our hearts break with pain.

The messages of divine heart's love became rules for enslaving the heart. We misused purest love to destroy life-energy. In the urge for power we were ready to betray divine love and thus also ourselves.

We have betrayed the part of ourselves that carries and sustains the most profound inner truth.

We have not betrayed Jesus or, as we often believe, God, because that is impossible. Rather, we have abandoned the divine part of ourselves because we were so blinded.

Jesus' whole life can be seen as a mirror for this part of ourselves.

The power he manifested is also inherent in us.

His deeds are signs of the strength of the heart's power that we can bring into life and of the endless and immortal love that we can allow to stream through us at every moment.

Jesus' death stands for the death of a part of us. It represents the moment when we could no longer sustain the power of the heart, when we pursued dominance and not the heart's love.

Jesus chose torture not to bring suffering upon himself but so that he might show us that we have betrayed ourselves and caused a separation. We were not ready to see the purity of the heart's power and even turned it, in the end, against ourselves.

The Resurrection symbolizes the moment when we will again be ready to see and accept purity of soul—the moment when we will again be ready to forgive ourselves, to sense love within us and for us once again, and thus rebuild the most profound trust in ourselves.

Oberweningen, May 14, 2003

Trust in ourselves? Of course we might say that we have already done so much to regain trust, and yet we have not dealt with the core of the injury.

We still do not want to look at the reason for betraying ourselves, to truly see it. So much fear still lingers in the background.

We are not just afraid of the power of religions, which is still actively present, nor are we only afraid of destroying the fictitious world and losing faith. Above all, we are scared of the deepest truth.

We are so terribly afraid of the truth, because we know perfectly well in our deepest core that we have long believed in something that was not and is not true. We believed in something that had been made into the only correct truth.

Through our beliefs, we constructed our world on the basis of this artificial truth.

Because we were intimidated by sin and an externalized God, we were ready to betray the heart's inner truth in order to adopt the truth of authority. This is exactly where the fear sticks within us—we are uncertain whether we can still trust ourselves.

We have deeply wounded our own souls, and that wound is far from healed. Betrayal, and especially fear of the betrayal, accompany us on the path throughout our lives. We cannot trust others and we cannot trust the world, because we cannot trust ourselves.

This wound, the heart, and the inner truth all need to be healed. They need more than just the excuse that all this belongs to the past and has nothing to do with us in the current reality.

It does indeed belong to the past, and yet it belongs to the present, too. It will also belong to the future if we are not ready to awaken the trust in ourselves again.

This is not a threat and should not be understood as such, because the time of threats and extortion is over.

The only possible path of development is to assume responsibility for ourselves and our own actions.

For too long, we have allowed our soul, our inner truth, our heart, and the divine in us to be limited and partially destroyed by presumed goodness of heart, by "truth" fabricated by greed for power, and by narrow rules.

The divine power that can ask anything of us other than to live out the love of our own hearts, cannot exist.

All rules, all restrictions, and all threats can derive only from addiction to power and command and not from pure, boundless heart's love.

Oberweningen, May 14, 2003

Any divinity that demands we relinquish our freedom may perhaps claim to be divine, but at its core it is still far from being heart's love and hence cannot be the divine eternal love. True connections—not only interpersonal relationships but also our most profound connection with divine power— develop on the basis of deepest trust.

When inner freedom cannot thrive and bloom, inner truth is also lost and buried. And when inner truth is forgotten, our essence is no longer alive. That means we are no longer who we are in our inmost being. This means we can no longer recognize our own strength and can no longer draw primal life-energy from our own source.

This is why it is impossible for the divine to take away our freedom. If it did, we would lose ourselves. As soon as we lose ourselves we can no longer be a pure bridge for divine power.

Why then would the divine demand that of us?

Such a demand can come only from someone attempting to take advantage of our inner power, or of ourselves as the representatives of this energy. It can come only from someone hungry for mastery over our heart's power.

Messages that originate in the heart's purest love cannot make demands. They cannot threaten; they cannot issue orders. They do not attempt to alienate us from ourselves. They cannot force us to do anything that would violate our life-energy, inner truth, and boundless freedom.

Love on demand is impossible; just so, love cannot demand.

How can it then be that messages received as instructions from Jesus or from God rudely demand that we relinquish the reins of our own lives? How can they expect us to give up our own freedom and inner will?

How it is possible that they attempt to stand above us with all sorts of threats? Why do they try to use the presence of sin to make us feel small and worthless? And how can they accuse us of being sinners who have lost God and faith, when our longing for the divine, our heartfelt desire for connection with it, is what makes us receptive to these messages in the first place?

If Jesus, as has been said, incarnated in order to embody the purest love and anchor it in matter, then it is impossible that his messages would not originate in this same divine love.

His purpose was not to get us sinful humans back on the right track. His role was not, and is not, to show us how we must live in order to achieve purity of soul. In that sense, he was not the preacher, who should bring us back into the fold like lost sheep. He could not do something like that because he carried love too deeply anchored in himself. He was too highly developed not to know that love can arise only from love and that the only possible path of development is the path of freedom.

He gave us the gift of the heart's purest love. Full of this heart's love, he exemplified how to manifest and live the divine love within, to preserve our intrinsic power and allow it to flourish. And what have we done to—and with—his gift?

Oberweningen, May 15, 2003

Of course we need discipline, if we want to connect to the divine and stay connected with it. But this is inner discipline that only we can define.

Impulses we get from those around us—from teachers, from books, etc.—offer valuable help and support, but they are still only impulses, not yet deeds, and we may not be really ready to integrate these impulses into our lives.

This is an aspect of the inner freedom that can lead to inner decision-making. No one else can decide for us, define for us or impose an inner discipline on us. Discipline that does not flow from inner desire has no value and no real power.

Discipline based on compulsion and fear is not discipline through which we can move from impulse to action and enter into connection with the divine, because it does not arise from inner truth.

Such discipline depletes a lot of our energy instead of enhancing it and supporting us.

The same is true of our connection to the divine. It gives us strength and has meaning only if it is based on deepest desire, on heartfelt longing for marriage to the divine.

Turning to the divine out of fear, habit, or—even worse—a bad conscience is unproductive, worthless.

We cannot connect with the heart's energy and divine love out of fear of sin. Fear and eternal love have such different vibrations that they cannot find each other and never meet. Similarly, we cannot find the divine within us if we seek it out of fear, reticence, anger, etc. Only through the heart and out of purest love can we experience the infinite divine power for which we are longing.

Piety—especially if it is only a pretense, which is unfortunately often the case—cannot help us if we do not carry the deepest longing for connection within us. We can feel this longing only out of ourselves, out of inner truth and deep honesty.

Compulsion and threats cannot be either the inducement or the basis for setting out on the truthful path of connection with the divine.

Oberweningen, May 15, 2003

Prayer that does not arise out of the heart's desire for connection with the divine and with all of creation cannot contain the spark—the clear and direct impulse—that could ignite the divine in us.

Without the heart's power, we cannot open our hearts and become receivers of divine love.

Clearly, fear of sinning cannot evoke this power of the heart. Fear cannot serve as the key to the heart. Fear takes us too far from our heart and from our center, so it loses the potential to accompany us to the source.

Prayers that arise from a feeling of smallness and helplessness also cannot lead us to freedom of the heart. Instead, they force us into dependency.

Feelings of unworthiness immediately put us in the position of sinners, driving us into poverty of heart.

By renouncing our own power and heart's love, we thwart ourselves; we are not able to open up and we certainly cannot receive.

Thus we cannot trust or be free. Without trust and freedom of heart, we remain wrapped up, alone in our own projections, instead of opening ourselves to the infinite and eternal power of life.

The result is often frustration, which cannot offer us any hope or comfort but only strengthens our sense of being small and worthless.

"...Because we are sinners, we cannot sense God, cannot connect with him. This privilege is reserved for the select few, intended only for those most deeply devoted to God. Thus our only option is to feel even more repentant, to be even more severe with ourselves, to obey the rules and follow the dogmas even more meticulously...."

We go round and round in circles without noticing that we are losing ourselves bit by bit. We give up our freedom of heart and cannot experience the divine.

Of what value, then, are the threats, pressure, and compulsion that are still used daily to get the "unbelieving masses" back on the path to God?

As already shown above, this is not the right way to experience the divine and anchor it in ourselves.

But do the religions really expect and demand that we unite with divine power to be able to live the heart's power? Is the way they show us and pressure us to follow truly the path of freedom that can lead us to the creation of inner strength?

Is it true that repentance can lead us to goodness and purity of heart?

By confessing our sins, can we really experience purity of soul and thus achieve the possibility of resurrection?

What stands behind all the threats and compulsion? Isn't it desire for dominance, something that wants us to subdue us and take possession of us and our power?

Is it really love that wants to destroy our freedom?

Is it really divine power that is attempting to separate us from ourselves and to make us fearful and reverent, to keep us away from the source?

Oberweningen, May 20, 2003

By allowing our life to be assessed according to standards, by accepting rules and frames determined from outside, we acquiesce and become dependent. We relinquish our power to guide our own life and strength.

We cannot relinquish our freedom of life and heart and at the same time pursue inner truth. Inner truth arises out of own personal freedom and can only unfold through the joy of life.

Strict rules, clearly defined sins, required repentance, and ceaseless threats deprive us of the possibility of developing—and especially following—our inner truth. The obvious consequence is dependency, because we no longer have the opportunity to choose and decide for ourselves.

Making our own decisions requires personal development because it challenges us to take sole responsibility for the path we have chosen. But we can really do this only if we are exempt from scolding, endless punishments, and the threat of being called sinners.

We alone can decide what is right for us and how. No one can make that decision for us, and it is even less possible for someone else to determine how we ought to live.

In the same way no one can define what sin is, because every attempt to do so immediately establishes clear limits that make personal decisions impossible.

The power of sin is used to contain us, to maintain control over us, rather than to help us to follow the path of development. Those who support dominance and force see the path of personal development as dangerous because it is not entirely predictable. Above all, it fosters individual freedom and thus freedom of heart, which clearly leads to independence and to reassuming leadership and responsibility for our own lives.

Sin has no meaning when we accept life as a process of developing and learning.

First, because the concept of sin prohibits too many possibilities, blocking some of the many possible paths from the very beginning.

And second, because sins are a burden that intimidate the joy of life, freedom, and life-energy. Thus they prevent connection with the divine power that is also a part of life-energy. Sins make it impossible for us to shape our own lives according to the principle of inner truth.

The idea of sin has power only because we have accepted the duality of life, because we have begun to distinguish between inside and outside, between good and evil, between ourselves and the divine.

Where there is no separation, there is also no possibility of being unfaithful to inner truth.

When we follow our inner truth, we cannot take the "wrong" path. Of course there are diverse paths, but they all lead through a learning process to further development of our lives.

When we see ourselves as part of the divine, we carry the divine within us. Consequently, it is impossible for us to carry sin against life within us.

But because we no longer see and feel ourselves as part of the whole, we forget that with our actions, regardless of their nature, we give others opportunities to learn, so we can tread the path of common development together.

Of course diverse decisions are possible, and they are not all beautiful and pleasant for everyone, but this does not mean that they are automatically sinful. Through diversity, we are able to learn and develop.

How can endless, divine love restrict us with sin, if it is supposed to support us on the path of development?

How can the divine demand that we be perfect and live without so-called sins? To learn to apply and direct our own energy through life, we must be able to experience the power of our own freedom and chosen actions.

Oberweningen, May 20, 2003

Connection originates from profound trust—trust that should result from both sides entering into communication, into exchange and connection. If trust were only one-sided, there would be no direct, targeted energy to create—and especially to maintain—the connection.

Trust means that we dare to open ourselves, to reveal ourselves, and to be ready to enter into an exchange. It means being absolutely fearless, above all without a fear of the one to whom we open ourselves when we connect with each other.

From fear, only separation can result. It is not a connecting energy, because it closes us, makes us absent, and cannot support us into openness. Whatever form our fear assumes, it prevents us from being free of projections and imaginations. That leads us away from freedom of heart and toward restriction.

Connection cannot develop out of inaccessibility. If we are not ready to step out of our own world, shut off our own projections, and free ourselves, we also cannot open up. We deprive ourselves of the opportunity to touch each other.

This situation is caused by old fears embedded so deeply in our bodies that they have become an inseparable part of us. We are no longer aware that we carry these fears within us, hold them tightly, feed them with our life-energy. We are least conscious of the fact that we obey and follow them religiously.

In fact, we may even become aggressive when someone tries to show us that these fears are still alive and well in us. We do not want to believe that they are still present.

Why this reaction? Because with our deepest being we know very well that this is true, and we are so surrounded by fears that we are even afraid of letting go of them.

We have turned fear into our "protector." We have assigned it the task of confining us within "protective" walls, thus eliminating the danger of opening ourselves, entering into deep connections, and possibly being hurt in the attempt.

We have built a thick "crust" around ourselves and fail to notice that we have thereby cut ourselves off from everything, even our own source.

By separating outside from inside, we have cut ourselves off from both. In that way we lost our ability to maintain the connection, to be the connecting bridge, and finally to be the connection itself.

Oberweningen, May 22, 2003

Because of inner separation, we opened the door to fear and accepted it as our escort. In doing so we voluntarily gave up our own freedom.

This moment was also the point of departure for the religions in which we placed all our hopes, thus giving up our freedom for good.

If we consider the background of this situation in greater depth, we can understand why religions established their foundations in this way and why we have come to accept them as our own.

As mentioned earlier, we fell into a profound state of separation and became entangled in fear. We felt that we were losing ourselves *in* everything while losing everything at the same time. The duality that gradually developed and the process of personal individualization simply reinforced this feeling. We felt at once hemmed in and lost in an endless expanse.

All this led us to search for something that would provide security, order, and a clear framework—something that could show us the direction for our path. We got what we were looking for in the form of religions.

Because our search was based on fear, of course we could not attract true love. Instead, we got something that could support our fear and the separation within us.

Connections based on fear cannot grow and develop into true connections, let alone connections of the heart, because their basis is tuned to the frequency of fear and not the heart's oscillation.

In that moment, we confused divine love with power-hungry religions. In our deepest longing for consolation, security, and support, we failed to realize that we were following fear. We were no longer capable of distinguishing between infinite, pure, divine power, which was present so strongly and clearly through Jesus, and religions that used us to their own advantage.

Fear and uncertainty, already powerfully present, could serve as just the right means of making us feel small and unworthy.

We were ready and willing immediately to bow our heads.

We took guilt on our own shoulders without even asking if we were really guilty and if so, of what. We accepted the burden that was loaded onto us as a "gift," because at least it gave us something concrete to hold on to.

All of a sudden we were so deeply implicated that we no longer even noticed the depth of our involvement. We had taken the step, made our decision in favor of blind obedience to what our religions told us.

In that moment, we developed trust in religions. We received a clear direction that developed into faith. It continued to grow and even crossed the line into euphoria in some cases.

Having taken this step so far, we were no longer able to reverse course. We no longer had control over our own power and thus could no longer pick up the reins we had relinquished freely.

We had given permission to do everything with us: to use fear and awe to make us so small we could no longer feel ourselves; to impose rules so clear and brutal that we could no longer really move; to suppress the last remnants of our freedom with the concept of sin; to limit us to such an extent that we were willing to follow a single, clearly prescribed path.

At that point, our will, freedom, and inner truth were subdued, and we no longer experienced the restrictions as extortion. Then we could be shown the beautiful face of our "Savior," who assured us we were still on the right track after all.

Oberweningen, May 22, 2003

No wonder we put ourselves in such a subordinate position, since we were no longer able to pursue our inner truth. We were no longer capable of holding on to our own energy and standing behind it.

As a result of the blindness—and, in part, the euphoria—with which we joined this stream, we did many things that we might not have decided to do on our own.

We invested our own energy, convinced that we were doing so in God's name and for the sake of universal advancement.

And in this way we did not notice that we and our energy were being manipulated. We did not realize that many things were done in God's name, but that God's name was also often misused simply to keep us in check. Having so recently discovered security in religions, we did not want to see what was happening to us.

All of this was our own decision; we were supporting the whole system voluntarily with our inner energy. Thus we cannot hold anyone else responsible; rather, it is up to us to discover what kind of impacts and consequences now remain within us.

Whether consciously or not, we are always accompanied by the reality that many of us not only participated in shaping this game ourselves but also brought many others under the sway of the religions.

We allowed ourselves to be dragged down and even pulled others along with us. We were ready to destroy and suppress life-energy. We did this to ourselves and demanded that others do the same.

We were also willing to destroy those who chose not to cooperate. We assumed the role of perpetrators and manipulators and actively participated in shaping the whole process.

For many of us, this reality is still a constant companion. It is so deeply imprinted on us that we can no longer trust and are afraid of misusing life-energy once again. We can no longer trust our own feelings and power because we still live under the oppression of these memories.

Although we are, on the one hand, inwardly aware of this situation, on the other hand our religions continue to use their power to reinforce it. So any impulse for change remains weak and powerless.

Messages brought to us human beings through Jesus continue to be misused on a daily basis.

Although they originated in the deepest and purest divine love, they are still being used to threaten us.

For many of us, they continue to enclose and confine inner truth.

Oberweningen, June 26, 2003

Through Jesus, it became possible to reconnect with divine power in a deeper way.

At that moment, we held the power of decision in our hands. We had choices about what do with this new connection and especially about what we would allow to grow out of it. Everything was open and ready.

The doors were open, and we had the opportunity to enter.

And what did we do? We chose the struggle for power instead of divine peace. Not only that, we were even ready to use and even misuse purest, divine energy and love in this struggle. We stood this clear, pure energy on its head, tore it away from its source, and adapted it to our self-serving plans. As a result, it no longer had anything in common with the divine or with primal divine love. We debased it, took its power and gave it a new form and new contents so we could apply it to our own struggle for power.

As we struggled in God's name for personal power and dominion, we transformed purest love into "swords of righteousness." Unfortunately, we did not notice that we had used these swords to cut the spiritual umbilical cord linking us to the divine, and we fell into a vicious circle.

We inflated this inverted energy like a balloon and gave it infinite importance and force.

Not only as individuals but also en masse, we fed this creature with our own strength, our potential, and our heart-energy. In our euphoria, we failed to realize what kind of course we had chosen.

Once imprisoned in this force, we could not simply withdraw from it.

Our will and our ability to make decisions had taken such a beating that we were no longer able to follow our inner intuitions and our own feelings.

We were (and still are) like travelers on a ship, so enthused with feelings of power, euphoria, and imagined piety that we failed to notice that the ship was destined from the outset to sink because its basic structure was unsound. This ship, built of misused and perverted divine love, was not and is not fit to ride the waves of life.

At first just a small boat, it eventually developed into a gigantic ship, although it still had no future. All its grandeur, refinement, and stability were simply imagined and false.

In the beginning was divine love. It was a gift to us, and we exploited it through our own will to power.

We stood in front of the fateful door that could have led us to connection with the divine, but instead we chose a different door, the door of separation.

Now we are standing in front of doors again.

The moment of decision has come again. Have we gained enough inner strength by now, and independent will to take a different step? Are we again ready to follow our inner truth and to connect with the divine in a new and different way? Are we ready to jump overboard and abandon ship in time to avoid sinking with it?

Have we freed ourselves sufficiently from the threat of sin and the power of ecclesiastical institutions to be ready to take a new step and seek a new connection with the divine and with all that exists?

Is experiencing and living divine love more important to us now than the security we found in the lap of religions?

Oberweningen, June 27, 2003

We now find ourselves in a situation and constellation very similar to Jesus' time.

We as humanity face the possibility of taking a very important step. It is a step that is important for each of us personally and at the same time for all together collectively as humankind.

This is an opening that could make us able to connect in a new way to all that exists. This also means a new level and a different intensity in our connection with the divine.

The intensity of energy and life in Jesus' time was similar to what we are experiencing now.

Of course we experienced it differently then, although the quality was similar, because humankind was at a different stage of development.

To experience this opening it was like we had to go through the eye of a needle: everything was as if compressed, intensified, and concentrated. At that time we could not stand the intensity of coming through that narrow passage into openness.

By perverting love's power, we cut ourselves off from the source and could not experience the true process of opening.

Now we are standing again in just such an intense phase when everything compresses to complete the passage and transition.

The whole process happens in a frame of a cosmic collaboration, which means that the transition is happening with planetary support. That's why the intensity is so clearly present and can make the process possible.

Everything is present at once, as if all of creation were revealing itself in one single point, manifesting as a help for the step that we, as the cosmic whole, can take.

Of course this is not exactly the same process that might have taken place in Jesus' time.

In the interim, we have undergone a lengthy training. We have landed in a reality different from the one we could have achieved then.

This is why we no longer need the immediate embodiment and anchoring of the divine in a concrete figure such as Jesus was then.

All those who open themselves can now carry this divine love, the Christ power, within.

We are now going through the process of building up the basis of our development as individuals.

In Jesus' time, we walked this path of the process in common, as humankind. Now we have traveled much farther along the path of personal individualization; we have internalized correspondingly more decision-making strength and will, and through these also responsibility.

Nonetheless, we are still traveling a common path as humankind.

We are momentarily standing in the preparation phase of a process in which we have opportunities to work through many issues, to forgive ourselves, and to let go of a great deal.

Because it is as if we were passing through an assortment of filters or a series of gears, and all of our "baggage" that we are carrying within us and with us is becoming increasingly apparent. We cannot take it all with us as we pass through the eye of the needle.

Therefore, in this first phase everything is becoming increasingly present one more time to give us the opportunity to sort out and reposition ourselves.

To go through this process, however, it is very important to be free of old patterns, tight matrices, old positions, outmoded ideas about sin, and old-fashioned threats. We are still clinging to outdated structures, energies and powers that cannot be involved in the new connection to divine love because they pull us exactly in the opposite direction.

Oberweningen, June 27, 2003

Regardless of how old we are, how we live, what we have already done and experienced, what level we are on, or how often we have reconfigured our lives, we are all challenged to create a new foundation during this preparatory phase.

It is not really a matter of creating but of sorting out and restructuring. The result will automatically be a whole new internal structuring and shaping of space.

It's like moving to a new house in a different town. We have an opportunity to handle all of our possessions and to decide anew what we want to keep, what we still need, what will really fit in our new home. We can also find out what kind of memories our belongings carry and which ones are significant for us.

The process is exactly the same when we translate the equipping of an outer into an inner space.

We cannot build a new foundation according to old rules, nor can we build it of old threats or out of fear of sin, because we would continue to bind ourselves to outdated forces and the perversion of life-energy. The old cannot support us in the new process of openness.

Of course this does not mean that we should reject Jesus' messages. It means we should make an effort to finally understand them correctly so that we can experience true, divine love through them.

At this point the question arises, why are Jesus' messages so important, although they came about in a different time?

As mentioned earlier, we now find ourselves in a constellation very similar to that of Jesus' time. In this way, we carry his true messages within us, along with the impulse of true, purest love. Essentially, we are tuning in to the same frequency again.

Jesus' true messages are messages of divine love. As messages of the divine, they are timeless and boundless.

Through our modern experiences, we can understand and receive messages differently than we would either tomorrow or the day before yesterday, but the messages are universal. For this reason, they are independent of and unburdened by time and space.

To experience this level of the messages, we often need to go through heaps of ballast and look behind the written words.

Through misunderstanding and misuse, these true messages have often been unfortunately so changed and perverted that we can no longer recognize the source.

Oberweningen, June 28, 2003

Religions as we know them today are not living religions. Their foundations are far in the past and have long been unable to support life-energy. As a result, they cannot develop new impulses for the progress that is needed.

We face a dead end because life-energy has been blocked—the life-energy we surrendered gradually to religions and to the power that stands above them.

Even if we free ourselves and stand on our own two feet, life-energy remains bound to the power of religions and is still in danger of being manipulated.

To free this life-energy, we should finally begin to live consciously the reality of the heart's power.

We could say we have forgotten what real heart's love is, what real life-energy is, or—in other words—what *heart* is, what *love* is, what *life* is, and what *power* is.

When we hear the word *heart*, we usually see in our mind's eye the image of a red heart or our feeling for the physical heart in our body.

By that we forget that the heart is the center of life. The heart is the holder of the highest power. The heart symbolizes the vibration of the divine within us.

The heart is the door to wholeness, to eternal unity. Only through the heart frequency can we really experience divine love in order to live it. We can philosophize, discuss, and meditate on love, life, and power, but all our efforts are in vain if we do not open our hearts. The heart is the key.

When we talk about *love*, we usually limit it to love between human beings, specifically, between two human beings, most often of opposite sexes, who are having an affair or are partners for life.

When we do so, we deny the biggest part of the spectrum that this power originally encompasses. We define a narrow corridor within which love is allowed to exist and to flow, and we reject all aspects of love that do not conform to this rule. Love is the power that flows through openness of the heart. It is true heart-energy, the energy we can activate with our hearts. Hence it is the energy we bring to life when we are ready to open the door of our heart.

Conversely, we use the term *love* for everything, higgledy-piggledy, without being conscious of what it really means.

We usually associate *life* with sleeping, working, eating, the difficulties we face, etc.—in short, with everything between birth and death. Here again, we are moving on only one level. Although admittedly important, this level is not all that life entails.

Life is the impulse through which everything came and comes into being. It is the background of all that exists, the impulse that is given to us and makes it possible for us to connect, through heart's love, with everything that lives and is.

Life is a great opportunity for us. Because life is given to us, we have the opportunity to bring true love into life, through our hearts, and thus collaborate actively and contribute to life.

The term *power* is usually associated with physics or with bodily strength, with the energy that allows us to accomplish something on the physical level. But we forget that we also need a different but equally real energy.

That is the power of creation, the energy from which life is drawn. This is the power that can carry the impulse of life. It is the basis of life, the basis of love. It surrounds us and is the basis of everything what we see, feel, love, eat, breathe, hear... of everything we are.

This means that power is the basis of life and life the basis of love.
Love can blossom only through life, with the heart as the key.
Love has no strength unless it can draw from the source of life-energy.
The heart cannot be effective without the power that flows through it in the form of life.
Likewise, love has no power if the heart is not receptive to the spark of life.
Life cannot flow if there is no power of the heart to awaken love.

Jesus' messages are all about the heart, about love, about life, and about power. There is nothing in them about sin, rules, threats, etc.

The divine in us is awakened through heart's love, which emerges from the life-energy that then keeps it alive.

Oberweningen, July 27, 2003

As long as we cannot recognize the divine within us, we also cannot see the divine in all the various forms around us.

We often hear that recognizing the divine in ourselves means seeing its reflection in us, but it actually means much more then that. It means really experiencing ourselves as part of the divine, being it and also living it.

When we just thirst for divine love and for the ability to be recognized by it, when we just long for an external God to appear and help us, when we just hold up God's image in front of us and visualize it, we place barriers between ourselves and the divine power instead of living and experiencing it within ourselves.

It is not enough to passively attract divine power, to look up to it, to worship it, if we are not also ready to actively live it.

Actually, we cannot attract it and activate it in ourselves if we do not allow it to flow through us and are not ready to accept it as part of us.

We live in a time when it is no longer possible to avoid responsibilities. If we do so, we cannot acquire the strength needed to act.

Without action, we cannot express our own deepest essence; we cannot bring our fundamental message to light, let the personal coloration of our life appear; we are not ready to find, recognize and share our personal treasure.

In that case, what is left of the meaning of life and of our presence in it? Who are we, if we cannot play and be our role? Who are we, if we blindly follow what is determined to be right yet we cannot remain faithful to our inner truth?

Somewhere along the way, we shifted God's image and the divine from within ourselves to outside. At that point, we began to see religions and all their close "servants" as embodying the divine or as a bridge to the divine.

In doing so, we relinquished our decision-making force to others. We were ready to obey everything and everybody because we believed that by doing so we were following the path of the divine.

Through the faith and belief that we were following the divine, we became willing to freely surrender our power, our life, our love, and our heart.

We thought this would free us from making decisions, which are often not easy to make.

We believed we would avoid the risk of deciding on the wrong path in life.

We also hoped to lay down our burden of uncertainty and fear.

But we did not notice that we had lost ourselves by doing so, because we gave away and denied our power of decision.

No one, not even God's servants, can make decisions for us. Nothing and no one can determine the way for us, even if that way is communicated to us in a sermon as a message from God.

If we are not ready and willing to recognize our own power of the heart as divine and to use it as such, everything around us can shout out the "divine" message that we are longing for and need at that very moment, yet we will not be able to hear it. Even though we want to, we will not be able to hear it, because *as long as we are not ready to live out the divine in ourselves, we cannot recognize the divine in general.*

We will not be able to recognize divine power, feel its presence, if we do not carry it within ourselves, because we can only live, experience, see, sense, and radiate that which we carry in us, that which we are.

Oberweningen, November 24, 2003

As long as we can decide freely, we "rule" our own power; as soon as we relinquish our decision-making capacity, we allow others to rule us.

We make our energy available. Through decisions, we determine the flow of our life-energy.

Deep inside, we are afraid of making decisions. We are profoundly afraid of opportunities to make decisions, because fear of being wrong, sinning, failing, losing the connection to the divine, not being divine, and so forth is so deeply embedded in us.

Through decisions, we set life-energy in motion and transform it into action. This is how we act and affect the image of life as a whole, by participating directly in action.

We handed responsibility over without a bad conscience because we thought we were putting our decisions "in safe hands." We have overlooked the fact that in this way we lost our own freedom.

Instead of being the fire itself, we are now the woodpile on the hearth, waiting for a spark from others to set us on fire.

We still have the potential to become a fire, but we depend on those who are ready and willing to provide the spark.

We can give away all we possess, give our entire inheritance to strangers, even give away our last shirt; we can spread love all around us, radiate love's energy, and so on, but in the end we will still be ourselves.

What we should not give away is the key to our own heart. If we lose that, we also lose the ability to steer our life.

We can recognize the heart's key and act out of it only when we are ready and willing to see ourselves as part of the divine.

If we separate ourselves from the divine, we deny the mystery and miracle of life.

Oberweningen, November 25, 2003

Life's greatest miracle is creation.

Existence has no end. Forms change and develop, but life remains living. It flows on unhindered in different forms.

Life is never lost and never breaks down. Life's creation carries eternity within itself.

Life is a cycle that can be pure infinity if it embodies the energy of creation.

When we are caught up in the flow of life, we are part of creation's energy and also part of the endless cycle. We have the opportunity to live life creatively and to be creative.

This does not mean that we must create new forms of life or invent or even create life itself.

Everything that is needed is already inherent in life. Life carries power, information, impulses, love, forms, light, matter—all things that we cannot invent or create.

What we are meant to do, however, is to open ourselves toward all of these in order to recognize them all. Only then do we get the opportunity to enliven them all, which is precisely our task.

At every moment, we have the opportunity to bring life's impulses and creations to light. This means that our personality, our existence, and our creative energy activate that which would remain passive without our presence.

Our source is life itself. We draw from the source of life so that we can be creative and make creation possible for life. Here again, we stand in the cycle of life. *We draw from the source to pour into the source. In this way we flow into the source and into life to be life itself.*

We need not rack our brains to create new and original inventions if we are ready and willing to open our hearts, to open ourselves, because in this way everything is present, and we stand at the source.

If we make the decision to flow with life in order to be creative, we no longer need to consider what is right and what is not. We can proceed directly to action.

In this case, we can draw from the source without detouring and connect directly to the force of creation.

The moment of decision plays a very important role in the creative process as a whole.

The act of deciding can be compared to standing at an intersection. We have several options. When we decide, we define which way we want to go. At the intersection, we cannot choose two streets at the same time, as we cannot lead in life two parallel lives or choose two paths.

The decision is the moment when we lay the foundation of our development, because then we decide to point and lead our energy in a specific direction.

We cannot live creatively if we are not ready and willing to decide in favor of the path of creation.

Oberweningen, December 9, 2003

We cannot live and work creatively as long as we are still feeding our fear of doing or being "wrong." This fear, which wears down the impulse for life at its core, cannot serve as the basis of creativity.

The foundation of creative life is trust. To act creatively, we should become receptive. If we want to open ourselves, we need to trust. We can trust only when we are free of the fear of being judged.

But who can judge us and our deeds if not life itself? Who has the power, the extensive insight into life, to have the ability and—ultimately—the right to judge us and determine what is right and what is wrong?

The only judge of life is life itself. Even life is not judgmental but is ready and willing to teach us and to learn with us.

We cannot choose the wrong way at the intersection because there is no wrong way.

When we are finally ready to recognize and accept this fact and allow it to take root in us, we will immediately be closer to a creative life.

Instead of pressuring ourselves with even more written or unwritten rules, we need to pay more attention to freeing ourselves. We need to completely free our own hearts from the fear of being judged, from inner uncertainty, and from mistrust.

Without this freedom, we cannot decide, which means we cannot act. And when we are incapable of action, we cannot support life in any creative way.

Wasting creative energy by hesitating and going round in circles is worse than deciding on a path that leads to a solution that may later prove not to be the optimal one. It is most important to act, to let our life-energy flow under our own direction.

We always have the option to decide again—to reorient ourselves, to do something different from what we did before—but we should not force the flow of life to a halt. That costs us a lot of energy, which cannot be used effectively, because it cannot serve the flow of life.

The power is in this case an absolute waste, similar to heating a house in winter with all the windows open, then complaining that it's not warm enough and turning up the heat.

We are just as dissatisfied with our life. Instead of being receptive to life through deciding to act so that we can shape life creatively, we often prefer to remain trapped in a vicious circle of fears, mistrust and block the flow of life.

All it takes is one single step to get the energy flowing again. That step is making a decision.

Oberweningen, December 10, 2003

Life's chief attribute is flow.

Life can be active only when it is flowing. When the flow of life is interrupted for whatever reason, life loses its living spark and the ability to be active and creative.

This means that everything that supports or wants to support internal life should go with the flow in order to really enliven life, live it, and draw from its source.

Our role is to carry and support life, to enable it to come to expression through us and to provide a form for life's creation.

We can do all this only when we are ready and willing to go with the flow.

Going with the flow of life means not clinging to anything, being ready to let go of everything at any moment. It means being flexible and staying flexible, being alert and open at all times. It also means being able to make decisions and to act, etc. To put it briefly, "let it flow."

Here, too, religion has usually taught us the opposite: we should be good and diligent and obey strict rules. We should look neither right nor left but just follow the one and only "right," prescribed path.

Decisiveness, capacity for action, and the very expression of the creation have been portrayed to us as the devil's seed, while we were told to stay within our own boundaries and remain small, undemanding, obedient, etc.

Whether we like it or not, however, life includes inherent challenges, multiple opportunities, and diverse paths. Thus we need courage, energy, independent will, joy, and satisfaction in life to experience life's creation.

Otherwise, we can experience only passive, arid life—like eating only the peel instead of the whole juicy fruit.

Any aspect of life we may choose to consider is based on flow.

Consider your body: it is obvious that it can only be and stay healthy as long as life and energy can flow through all its parts.

Any blockage means that life-energy—"life nourishment"—cannot get through. Where this happens, energy is imprisoned, used up to maintain the blockage instead of to nourish the body. Such blockages come about because we are not ready to let go, to decide, because we often stay beside instead of in the flow of life.

If we see love as an expression of life, we can realize that it has power only when we are ready and willing to let it flow. If we attempt to hold it fast, it is weakened and lost.

This is clearly reflected in relationships, whether partnerships or friendships. They remain alive only as long as we are willing to go with the flow; to stay flexible, free, open, and alert; and to be mature enough to let go. All of these are attributes of flow.

As soon as we impose strict boundaries and unnecessary rules, we attempt to hold love and life-energy fast. Obviously, this interrupts the flow.

This usually happens because we are not ready to grow, because we are afraid, because we do not want to make decisions, because we forget how to enjoy life or how important it is to let it flow.

Let's look at money as another expression of life. To have power in our lives, money has also to flow. Having money in itself, we do not have anything yet. If the important thing were to possess money, to have it in hand, we could make our own money out of paper and it would serve the purpose just as well. Homemade money is just as valuable as money that is not allowed to flow.

Money becomes valuable only when we are ready and willing to let go of it, to contribute it to the flow and cycle of life.

As these examples demonstrate, it is impossible to hold fast to anything in the flow of life. It is even less possible to cling to the flow of life itself.

We need too much energy for this, and above all, it takes all the joy out of life.

Oberweningen, December 13, 2003

What do we gain from life when it's no fun anymore, when we cannot enjoy it? What good is it to have the juicy fruit before our eyes and chew only on the tasteless peel? What do we get out of the fruit if we are not allowed to eat it? What do we get out of life if we cannot or are not permitted to enjoy it?

Satisfaction and joy of life are the driving forces we need in order to work creatively and actively co-create life.

It is not the money we can earn with our activities; it is not the success we can achieve; it is not the acknowledgement that might come to us through our work, etc.—it is joy in life that gives us the strength to continue our path, our development, and to continue to serve life.

If there is no space in our life for the joy of life, we lose the energy that provides the foundation in building our life.

We cannot set life-energy and the flow of life in motion or let them flow through us if we cannot be delighted with this process, if we do not know real, primal and pure joyfulness of life, if it cannot live within us, unfold and find expression through us.

The religions have made repeated attempts to show us that enjoyment and zest for life are unnecessary, that they simply corrupt us and make us lose our way. Moreover, religions even teach us that we are living in sin when we enjoy life. They show us repeatedly, in all-too-clear images, that delight and pleasure of life are nonsense and even poisons.

They have done everything possible to suppress the enjoyment of life in the bud.

As indicated earlier, this is also an expression of lust for power, a drive to shape human individuals into fearful masses that would be flexible, obedient, without will; and to use their power to serve its own desires, its own aims, and above all its own force. How else can we understand and explain this? To deny, suppress, and declare a sin our driving force, our fundamental energy?

How else should we understand it when part of life and thus also part of infinite love is shown to us as a sin and forbidden? This can only be an obvious attempt to force us away from the source, to prevent us from drawing pure life-energy out of it and being free and creative.

Of course our actions, work, and the "monuments" we construct are important, but they cannot develop on stable foundations if they do not grow out of zest for life or if we are not permitted to use satisfaction in life as a driving force.

They will be arid and devoid of life-energy, out of tune with the flow of life, not really living and forceful, because they cannot support the creation of life.

Oberweningen, December 15, 2003

Having made death the ruler of life is one of our major obstacles. Instead of being part of life, death is reigning over all of it.

Life is an unbroken flow. Even death, which we can understand as being born again into the spiritual sphere, is part of this flow of life. Without this part, there could be no birth into the physical sphere.

When we give death a gray mask or even a black one and separate it from the cycle of life instead of seeing it as part of it, we interrupt life's eternal flow.

In this way life-energy is lost instead of being carried on and moved forward, because the cycle of life is no longer complete. This gap in the cycle is due to the idea and image that death is the end of life.

We would probably live life differently if we were free of the idea of death as blackness, a gray ending, a horrible hole waiting for us. This idea is like a heavy axe hanging over our heads, eternally ready to react to our every mistake.

Diverse religions taught us that if we avoid sin, diligently and virtuously follow the prescribed path, and obey the rules, we need not expect a horrible end to life.

Similarly, it was shown to us that horrors await if we do not abide by the "rules of the game."

These threats are so deeply imprinted on our souls in childhood that our courage to live life creatively is taken from us at the very beginning.

This is how we allow fear of death to gain power over us. At the same time, we fall on bended knee before those we believe to have a direct connection to the divine, whom we believe will be able to help us avoid the gray ending.

We are ready and willing to give up our freedom, to betray our inner urge to shape life creatively, and even to renounce our enjoyment of life. This clearly shows how deeply this fear has become rooted in us. Death is our "antagonist," our "enemy," and in this way our whole life becomes a fight against it.

In all this, we forget that death is originally actually a part of life—which means we are basically fighting against life itself.

How can we live life, go with the flow, and be part of the cycle of life if we are fighting against these very actions, if they are our enemies? And finally, how can we trust life if, deep within us, we see it as our antagonist?

How can we still trust ourselves; how can we believe and trust others? Can we still trust anyone at all? "Yes, those who serve the divine"—because they forged the strong ties that bind us to the religions.

As soon as we can recognize and accept death as a part of life again, instead of as a gray or black abyss at life's end, the cycle of life will be whole again and thus also infinite and eternal.

Then life will be able to flow again, and we will flow with it.

Death, the end, life, and even ourselves, instead of being treated as opponents in a struggle, will once again be part of the whole and thus also part of us.

Then we will no longer need anyone else to mediate the connection to the divine for us, because we will again recognize the divine in ourselves.

We can achieve inner peace only then when we are ready and willing to see ourselves as creative expressions of the divine and thus as gifts of life.

Oberweningen, December 16, 2003

We can accept and enjoy life's gifts only when we are content with ourselves and our life. Only then we are really and truly in the flow of life, and only then can life flow through us.

When we live life, we are a gift to life and at the same time we are a gift from life.

We make it possible for life to express itself through us, to implement part of its creative composition through us.

We are also a gift because through our existence we impart, radiate, and distribute our most profound inner message, which we carry stored in our deepest being. This message gives coloring and diversity to the flow of life.

We can pass on the message of life only if we really live it. Only in this way do we give our own power a foundation and expressive possibilities.

To live and experience our own message, we should first find peace in ourselves and make peace with ourselves. Otherwise we cannot even "hear" the message, let alone bestow any creative energy on it.

To make peace with ourselves means to accept ourselves as we are. This means knowing, accepting, and living with all aspects of ourselves. Otherwise, we cannot be this whole message and thus the gift.

Our personal message is and remains eternal. It is bound to time and space only through us and will never get lost.

We are often driven through life by a panicky feeling of being unable to fulfill our life's task. We cannot live calmly and in inner peace because we are either stuck deep in the past or focused on the distant future.

We analyze and dissect our whole life and every situation to finally understand what is happening, how and why. We are always searching for reasons, errors, and new opportunities. In our constant attempts to be always better, we do not notice how good we are just as we are.

It is very important to be free of pressure and panic and to be conscious that our personal message is part of the eternal cycle.

Our message is present when we live it, when we are active in life. It becomes passive if we do not allow it to live or if we are not anchored and incarnated in the physical body.

But even at times when we cannot live our message or choose not to do so, it persists and bridges the passive phase.

Whenever we either experience pressure or pressure others, we cannot radiate the energy of our personal message. Not being able to do that, we soon begin to feel useless, unnecessary, unworthy, meaningless, and unloved, as if life has no more meaning.

In this state, we no longer see ourselves as a creative part of life; we cannot enjoy life anymore; we cannot recognize the divine in us, and in this way we interrupt the flow and cycle of life.

In such moments, we begin to look for hands that represent the connection and bridge to the divine. We begin to project energy outside of ourselves and to give control over our own power into the hands of others. Unfortunately, such situations are often misused. Instead of offering real help, those who hope to gain our energy for themselves offer only consolation.

In such moments, the basis of dependency develops.

We can help others rediscover the flow, close the circle of life, and seize their own power again. But we cannot go with the flow for them, or hold the cycle of life together with our own energy. Even less can we receive their power for them—because in this way we would be the one who would flow with the stream of life, using their power for ourselves, etc., and those who sought help would sink even deeper into their own frustration and pain.

Oberweningen, December 17, 2003

For the most part, unfortunately, religions and churches were designed to keep individuals in fetters by making them dependent.

When this happens, the heart's power cannot serve as the guiding force that maintains and nourishes connection. Instead of pure love, the guiding force is often an egotistical feeling of self-interest.

That cannot be a real help, able to restore profound hope and provide a supportive ground beneath our feet. All promises of help are thus flimsy and hollow, because they have no background and no foundation.

Help based on real love helps the seekers rediscover their own source and join the flow of life and creation again.

Help of this sort helps a hiker to find the path he was looking for. It does not try to persuade him to follow its own path for reasons advantageous to itself.

If we are truly ready and willing to help, we also know that our own wishes and needs should remain in the background so that we can act out of the heart's purest love.

Religions, churches, and spiritual teachers should not attempt to be the pillars of the temple, let alone the temple itself. They ought to help us erect or rediscover the pillars of our own temple.

They should not be the source, but should help us rediscover our own source.

They cannot help us by attempting to draw from the source on our behalf instead of showing us how we can draw life from it ourselves and find our own access to it.

They also do not help us if they go into the flow of life on our behalf but are not ready or willing to teach us how to swim with the flow.

They may fetch the stars down from heaven for us, but it does us no good if we don't learn how to do it for ourselves in future.

Above all they cannot serve as a bridge to the divine if deep within themselves they do not want us to establish this connection ourselves. They should be ready and willing to let go, with open hearts, once we have taken this step alone.

Otherwise, our experience is like brief flashes of light that are not sustained by the constant flame of life but only by the addiction to more fireworks. They satisfy our hunger briefly but do not provide the real food we need as a basis for life.

Unfortunately, the major religions are based on addiction to rapid gratification, to these brief bursts of energy.

If we read the texts that we rely upon to translate and convey Jesus' messages, we can very clearly perceive that they do attempt to really teach us how to live so that we become creative expressions of life. Instead, they attempt to show us that we are sinners and thus not part of the divine. They are efforts to engender longing for the divine in us, to make us a falsely generous offer of externalized divinity. They attempt to make us dependent on the crumbs they drop.

In such "games," unfortunately, we rapidly forget that we have the source within us, that we are the fire that can burn with full force, that we carry the divine in us, that we can live creatively and allow pure love to flow through us, etc.

We do not need to lick the empty plates and eat the crumbs that fall to the floor.

We have earned the right to draw from life with a big spoon.
We are mature enough to live creatively.
We are worthy to experience the divine living in and through us.
We bear within us the power of life and love, and are entitled to use them without restrictions.
We need no validation to do all this.
We also do not need anyone to do it for us.

Sometimes we simply need a hand to give us hope and show us our own path again. But our openness is too readily misused, and we are enslaved by self-described goodness of heart.

Oberweningen, December 20, 2003

We were given hope to keep us on track in our own life, not to make others dependent on us.

To be a reality, hope needs our life-energy. Without this energy, hope remains ungrounded, often a mere illusion—just information, just a thought or a wish, just an open door. It cannot lead us further if we do not choose to enter. Hope needs to be integrated into life. Otherwise it is like a dream with no dreamer, a motor without oil, a car with no driver, or a fruit consisting only of the husk.

We cannot construct life on the basis of hope, but we do need hope to construct life.

Hope gives us strength to draw from life, to continue to trust ourselves to take the next step. Hope can show us the way and encourage us to shape our life with verve and optimism.

Lifeless hope, however, soon turns to confusion and leads us to a dead end. It takes away the life-energy we need to sustain it, instead of guiding us to the source of life and giving us energy for life.

False hopes can take us to places in life that our soul never intended. This is especially true of hopes we take over from others or that have been strongly imprinted on us from our surroundings.

Unfortunately, we can very easily misuse hope as an effective means of manipulation. We can easily hide behind hope, a pretty face that ensnares others.

This is especially dangerous because our prisoners only notice that they have landed in a trap when it is already too late. Deeply confused and far from their own life source, they have only hope and arousers of false hopes to depend on.

Religions offer hope through the belief that we will enter the Garden of Eden after death and thus experience enlightenment.

This hope forces us into passivity and dependency because we immediately forget that we are meant to live life as Paradise and to experience enlightenment through our presence in life itself.

Hope of this sort leads us away from the source, toward unreality and illusion. It takes us out of the path of our life-plan. It seduces us and leads us astray, away from the flow of life. Clearly we are being manipulated along with our energy.

So we find ourselves in a trap. No matter how loudly we scream for life, no matter how much we pray and beg, believe and repent, we will be still stuck in the cage of bondage as long as we focus our life-energy on false hope.

Šempas, January 2, 2004

Who can possibly deliver hope by promising us Paradise after death? What right does anyone have to deprive us of the opportunity to achieve Paradise in life? To whom do we give such absolute power? We are told we will deserve and experience happiness only after death. Why are we ready and willing to see this threat as a hope held out to us? How can we be so blinded that we are no longer willing to see the truth? Why can we no longer distinguish hope from greed for power? Why can we no longer separate hope from the cage of bondage?

How can we allow ourselves to be made small and unimportant? How can we allow our wings to be clipped? How can we accept having the doors closed on our chances of finding power, courage, and the way to the light during life?

And more: why do we believe and blindly trust those who close the door in our faces?

Do we really not notice that those who call themselves our guides deliberately shut the door to the entrance—or do we choose not to see that?

Why don't we see it? Is it really only our profound trust in the churches or religions, or is it the underlying fear of being abandoned, of even losing ourselves, of not finding the "right" way? Or is it the fear of what might confront us if we decided to choose our own way?

Or is it perhaps a feeling of security and certainty, a guarantee?

A feeling that we cannot be wrong as long as we simply follow others and need not decide for ourselves?

A feeling that someone is standing behind us, looking out for us and even protecting us?

The time for such following blindly is over!

Blind following is much too limiting to show us the way.

It takes too much of our freedom to really help us continue.

It is restricts us too much to be able to give the breadth that we need for our further development.

Thus we are being held back, delayed, and blocked so that we can go no farther. Can this then really be the path of development? Is this really a help, or is it more of an obstacle on the path we as souls are attempting to follow?

We cannot, and most of all we need not sorrow and suffer any longer under heavy burdens or even feelings of guilt from the past.
At any moment, we have the option to do something good for the future.

Churches and religions attempt to label us sinners because we have not and still do not recognize Jesus Christ, God; because we were not advanced enough to follow him and acknowledge his deeds; and because we were and still are not ready to follow his will. So we were abandoned by him. Because we still have regrets about this, we are stuck in the past. We cannot take the decisive step to develop our own connection to the divine. Hence the door is shut.

We cannot see the light when we only want to see darkness.
We cannot be happy when we are inwardly convinced that we deserve only suffering.
We cannot make Paradise a reality during life when we believe that we are only allowed to experience it after death.
It cannot be otherwise, because we do not want to open the door; because we harshly see only what we allow ourselves to see; or because we even allow others to determine what we ought to see and are allowed to see.

Thus we close the door on ourselves.

Oberweningen, January 16, 2004

The divine, or God, has not abandoned us. We shut ourselves off, and were no longer ready to enter into connection. We did so because the conviction had been foisted upon us that we had betrayed and abandoned the divine.

We are not sinners; we have done nothing wrong. We simply lived and reacted in each moment as permitted by our level of maturity and the processes we were engaged in. Our actions supplied exactly the right training for us. This is still the case, so we are still not sinners.

Of course we are always seeking and experimenting. We are on our path of development and have not yet reached the goal. We are travelers involved in an ongoing process, subject to eternal challenges.

This is precisely why we need the freedom to explore different paths and lifestyles and to make "mistakes" on occasion. But this still does not mean that we are sinners abandoned by God.

It is our nature, human nature, to be active in an endless cycle of development; to pursue the process of being; to seek out life's challenges; to explore life, love, and the power of the heart in order to learn and thus to grow.

This is our nature, but we could also say that it is our task or role. We are not here to stay in one place and passively wait for something to happen. If we do so, we lose life-energy, much-needed hope, the supportive love of life and joy, and the creative power of life. In this way it becomes impossible for us to be explorers of life, which is exactly what we are by our nature.

No one can require us to change our nature, our fundamental basis, and our essence, let alone declare us sinners because we follow our own nature.

How can we endure this predicament? On the one hand we want to develop faith by obeying religions, because we wish to be in connection with the divine.

On the other hand, whether we like it or not, we are explorers of life by our very nature.

Because we trust religions, we also begin to believe we are sinners simply because we want to explore life creatively and actively.

Thus we are indirectly forced to give up our nature. But we cannot forget our primary nature completely. In spite of all our actions and efforts, it will always surface again.

This means that we are engaged in a constant inner struggle. We wish to experience the divine yet do not want to let go of religion. But we also cannot deny, conceal, or blot out our nature.

What shall we do now? If we want to experience the divine, we are not allowed to be sinners, yet we cannot survive without being allowed to live out our nature. We are pressured, forced to decide on a path.

But is this choice really necessary? Is it really not possible to experience both in our lives? Is there no way to combine these two paths instead of tearing them apart?

Perhaps the problem lies in the fact that we have made religion into a path. This means that we have gone so far as to elevate the original faith, which was not a path in itself, to the level of dogma. Suddenly, instead of being our accompanier on the path, religion became the path itself.

Instead of remaining an aid to establishing and maintaining our connection to the divine, the religions assumed power over this connection and thus also over life.

The original task of faith and religion was to accompany us, to provide spiritual instruction and support on the path and not to determine the path for us.

Pressuring us to stay on a defined track was not part of their role, nor was violating our inner nature, our inner desires, our hope, our joy in life, or our will in order to control us.

Our companion on the way has become an absolute leader who uses not only constructive means but often even hard threats and seductive yet empty hopes to keep us on track.

Is what we got really what we were asking of our faith and our religions? Didn't we only want help in reestablishing our connection to the divine? Wasn't our deepest longing only to become one with everything and thus part of creation? Weren't we searching only for security, shelter, support and company on the way?

Have our inmost hopes, our "naïve" openness, our deepest trust, and our obvious longing been used and perhaps even misused?

Oberweningen, January 17, 2003

If this is so, why do we still so blindly trust churches and religions? Where do we find the strength to continue participating in and even supporting them when there is so much that we no longer like and that no longer fits? Above all, why do we do this?

Are we really acting only out of fear of losing our way alone on the path out of the desire for security?

Are we really acting only out of the habit of clinging to someone, somewhere?

Or are we maybe already so dependent that we can no longer stand on our own two feet?

We are so deeply embroiled in religions and all of the appurtenant rules, in feelings of guilt, in the principle of sin, and in feelings of remorse, that we do not even notice it any more.

Even if we do not want to abide by the "rules," principles and hopes of a specific religion or follow its path, we remain part of it. The presence of religions is so deeply rooted in our civilization that we automatically follow them whether we want to or not.

They are so deeply embedded in us, so immovably rooted in our personal history and the history of humankind, that we cannot possibly run away or look away. We are part of them, and they have become part of us.

Accusations hang over us that we are sinners, that we are losers, that we have strayed from the path, that we are not good enough.

Threats hang over us that we will never achieve connection with God or the divine, that even after death we will sense and regret our sins. We are forbidden to enjoy life, to love our bodies.

All these threats are so dense, so present, so deeply and clearly embedded that they influence us whether we think and feel in this way or not, whether we believe them and give them our attention or not. We are caught in the net.

This is why it is so important to consider what underlies our faith and the religions. We should decipher the whole, understand it in our hearts and digest it deep within ourselves so that we can make new and more conscious decisions with a free heart and on the basis of our inner truth.

The time has come when we once again have this opportunity to make a new decision.

Looking back is no longer so important; now we must look forward.

Only in this way we will have the strength to see our faith and religions again as a companion, not as our sole leader. Thus we can also again recognize the true faces behind the masks and again sense and receive true messages.

And yet, to be ready to take this step, we should also be ready and willing to lay aside our own masks, get to know our own true faces, and allow our own truth to live. Otherwise we cannot stand independently on our own two feet. But this is exactly what we should do to activate the strength needed to take this step.

Through this new inner attitude, this inner search for our own qualities and own source of life, through this inner openness and willingness, through pure longing for truth and the inner faith that develops out of it, we can once again accept "outer" faith and religions as our trusted friends and important companions on the way. We can do so without experiencing fear and without falling back into the trap of bondage and dependency.

This can serve as the true basis for our common path forward—the path that allows trust to truly be trust, love to be understood as love, life to be accepted as life, and power to be used for building together, not for building up a one-sided empire.

Oberweningen, January 19, 2004

Such a connection can develop only on the basis of trust. And for real trust, we all need to be on the same level so we feel like equals.

If we are treated like dependent, disobedient children who are always being scolded, we automatically fall into the role of inferiority.

We are always being shown how far we are from our goal, how far we are still from communicating independently with the divine, how far we are still from paradise.

But it is not understood that this is what prevents us from achieving our goal. We have been kept back so that we can almost reach it, but we certainly cannot hold it, let alone truly experience and live it. All we can do is long for it.

In this way we become obedient and are ready to do everything we can to at least preserve some hope of being able to reach it in the future.

Because of this dependency demanded by religions, we cannot become self-reliant. Because of the threat of sin that forces us to the ground, we cannot develop strength for growth. Because we are forced to experience regret, which binds us firmly to the past, we cannot build up our future. Because of the constant scolding and frequent attempts to make us feel small and suppress us, we cannot see, let alone live out of, our own greatness and our own individuality.

God and the divine are depicted, in the messages through which we know them today, as an angry father who is never satisfied with us. We can never be good enough for him, regardless of what we do and how we do it.

Our strength and qualities are thus often overlooked and disregarded. Simultaneously, a finger is always raised to point out our weaknesses. More time and energy are spent pointing out the danger, our sins, possible dead ends in life, potential errors, etc. than in showing us life's beauty and the great opportunities for practice that our life's path offers us at every moment.

We do not need to know which way is wrong for us, because we will discover that simply by living it. We also do not need anyone to tell us which path we should decide upon, because we alone should bear responsibility for that decision.

What we could, however, use are recommendations on how to experience as much as possible in this vast field of opportunities. Above all, we could use advice on how to immerse ourselves more deeply in life in order to grasp its essence. How can we sink deeper into the power of the heart so we may really sense pure, true love? How can we make our hearts so free that we can always go with the flow of life and love? We need instruction in how to channel our energy into the constructive power of love instead of into power struggles.

Above all, we need to know not only how to understand all this but also how to apply it and live it in our daily life.

Again, we need faith of a sort that can serve us as a companion on the way and can make our life even more beautiful, mellower, riper and more vital. We do not need someone goading us along or keeping us constantly under control by calling us sinners.

This simply crushes us instead of offering support and providing opportunities for us to grow and to blossom.

Oberweningen, January 20, 2004

It is up to us to take the step into freedom. It is up to us to rediscover the path to independence. We are the only ones who can find this path for ourselves. We cannot wait to have it pointed out to us.

The time is past when we could wait for everything to be dished up on a platter for us. We have proceeded too far along the path of development to allow ourselves anymore to be pushed through life, manipulated like marionettes.

No matter how badly we may sometimes want it, there is no path to lead us back to the past. We also cannot spend a long time turning in circles and going nowhere. The path always continues, and thus our development continues. It is not possible to halt the process of growth.

We should be glad that this is true. We should continue on our way full of joy and enthusiasm for the wonder of life. Otherwise we stay attached to the umbilical cord, always trying to turn around and look back.

We should stop having a bad conscience about wanting to enjoy life and live it fully.

It is time to leave the security of the "parent's lap" and make a clear separation. We have spent enough time under the "wings of the mother hen." We have come so far that we no longer need this protection. On the contrary, the nest has become too small, too confining, too oppressive for us.

We have grown up.

We thus need freedom and challenges of life. We cannot be protected and cared for in this way any more. We can also no longer tolerate being scolded for what we do. We have set out on life's broad path and are free to decide for ourselves.

Of course this does not mean we must throw out everything we've learned or bury it in the cellar. But we are free to decide on our own what we want to keep and how to integrate it into our life.

Just as we would thank our parents when we grow up and are ready to leave the comfort of the nest, it is time to express cordial thanks to the religions for all the opportunities, experiences and support they offered us, and for their boundless love. But we can no longer cling to them. Above all, we cannot allow them to cling to us and prevent us from discovering our life's path.

The time is ripe and we are ready to take this step.

What are we still waiting for? Do we need specific permission to go our own way? Isn't this our right and even our obligation, to tackle our own role in life?

Are we not free to decide? The religions and churches always appeal to our freedom of heart and soul, so we can afford to take this step with a clear conscience.

We ought to listen first and foremost to our own soul and follow its impulses.

We ought to sense and know our needs, our hopes, our desires, our tasks in life.

Only then can we see what the religions can offer us in terms of support.

The religions should be there to support us in our decisions, our hopes, and our life tasks, and not to define them for us.

Again, we can compare this tie to the relationship between parents and their children. Parents cannot determine the path for a soul that has decided to incarnate as their child. They also have no choice about the destiny this soul brings with it and what it has resolved to learn in this life. They cannot select and determine the opportunities that will be necessary in their child's life. They cannot change the course or even the end of their beloved child's life, although it may be brutal and bloody.

How then would it be possible for them to change the soul's deepest nature?

Regardless of their wishes, parents accompany their child only for a certain time. During this time, they can offer protection and security; they can beautify and improve the nest; they can make their best efforts to do everything for their child. And yet they still cannot change the child's path. They have no right to do so, nor do they have the power to effectively intervene in the course of a soul's life.

Freedom of soul and freedom to decide our own path in life exists regardless of whether we are newborns on this Earth or experienced adults.

We, and only we, are able to decide which paths our souls will take.

We retain this authority over our decisions only as long as our lives fully embody our life-energy and connection to the source of life, and only as long as we do not relinquish our own energy and our power of self-determination to someone else.

Parents cannot keep their children from further development in life. Whether or not they let their children go freely, the children will find ways to discover their individual possibilities and to experience life's creation. Leave-taking between children and parents can be very beautiful if it is seen as an enrichment, as an opportunity to take the relationship to a new level.

But of course it can also be painful if it is seen as an ending, especially if we choose not to accept it. Parents should be ready to relinquish the role of escort and accept the role of a friend or perhaps advisor.

No other aspects of our complex situation are of concern to the religions and churches. We have reached the point where we should take responsibility for our own paths. We no longer have any direct need for teachers, nor should we continue to use other people's decisions to orient ourselves.

We are mature and ready to go our own way, which does not mean that we want to abandon religions. The point is merely to transform the connection and to change the roles religion has played in our lives. The relation is all that is changing.

We are independent now, standing on our own two feet. We want to decide for ourselves, and as a result we are also ready and willing to bear the responsibility alone.

Thus we are also ready to let go.

But does wanting to be independent make us sinners, nonbelievers, or even enemies of the religions or churches?

Are adult children sinners when they leave their parents' home?

Are we sinners for wanting to change out of clothing that has become too small, too tight for us?

Are we sinners for attempting to remain true to our development, our growth and our soul's path?

Oberweningen, January 22, 2004

Some may consider us sinners, or behave as if we are sinners. That certainly does not mean that we are really sinners.

This labeling has power over us only when we see ourselves as sinners, when we are ready and willing to accept that we sin by remaining true to our souls.

Because then we will also accept living as sinners, which means that we no longer embrace life in its full power and lushness, that we no longer allow ourselves to enjoy life, that we are no longer ready and willing to recognize our own greatness, that we no longer choose to acknowledge our own value and the value of our role in life.

Sin is strongly associated with feelings of remorse. If we feel remorse because of sins, we curtail, reduce, and shorten our enjoyment of life—which means we limit the flow of life-energy, love, and the power of the heart. We may not really want this to happen or do it consciously, but it happens automatically because the connection between our heart's power and the flow of life is very tight.

As a result, we will become weaker because we are no longer completely filled with life-energy.

Just as a half-empty balloon cannot rise high, we cannot make our way through life appropriately and powerfully if we live with reduced energy.

We may not be excluded from life, but in all likelihood we will become passive because we no longer have access to the energy needed for active living.

If we cannot or do not want to open our hearts as wide as we used to, we cannot open ourselves to divine love or to the divine itself to the same extent, and thus the connection fades.

Of course we might argue that remorse brings us closer to the divine and that its very purpose is to strengthen and stabilize our connection to the divine by reducing our attachment to enjoying life and its sensual pleasures.

We might also say that the divine is not directly associated with love, anyway, and is therefore not dependent on openness of heart and the flow-through of life-energy.

But is that really so?

Isn't the power of the Christ a quality or specific frequency of power of the heart?

What is the divine if not purest love?

What is God if not creation's power of the heart?

How can we imagine God and how shall we experience the divine, if not as a flow of love?

How is it altogether possible to separate life from the divine and how is it possible to separate love or the heart's power from life?

Is it possible at all?

What is left of life-energy if we exclude love?

What remains of the divine at all if we extract the heart's power, or the heart's love?

The divine is the creative power of life.
Life is love's power of the heart.
Love is the divine power of life.
Life is creation.
Creation is the divine in us.
We are an expression of love, and love is an expression of the heart.
The heart's power is our life-energy.
Life-energy is the creative reflection of life in us.
We are the reflection of divine power of the heart.

The heart's power is nourishment for creation.
Creation is nourishment for life.
Through creation, life-energy is our nourishment.
Nourishment emerges from divine love.
Love emerges from openness of heart.
The heart needs openness to be divine love.

We need openness in order to receive divine love and interweave it creatively into life.

We cannot separate love from life, life from power of the heart, the heart from the divine, the divine from creation, creation from us human beings. It is impossible, because each is empty and powerless without the other and simply cannot exist.

We live in illusion when we think that we can experience connection with the divine by renouncing life.

And, if we are told that we can only connect with the divine if we experience remorse for our sins and thus regret our deeds and the past, that is a blatant lie.

Oberweningen, January 25, 2004

The possibility of allowing creative energy to flow into life develops out of abundance.

Abundance has its source only in a forthright attitude and inner joy in life, and above all in openness of heart.

Creation is the expression of our connection with the divine. This means that our connection with divine energy—with the heart quality of Christ's power, or with the divine itself—rises from our own abundance.

And when can we say that we feel, experience, and live life's abundance?

When we feed the feeling of being sinners who have abandoned God and are therefore meant to lead a life of remorse?

Or is it when we are happy, satisfied with ourselves and with life, when we can enjoy life and devote all of our energy to our own task of life?

Abundance means fullness. It means being so imbued with life-energy that we can radiate enjoyment of life. It also means having both feet on the ground, being well grounded in life, and finding peace in ourselves and our body. Above all, it means being at peace with ourselves. In this state, we can pursue our inner truth, and remain true to our own souls and to the path we have chosen.

Abundance does not mean having to renounce life and creep into our "shells." It does not mean viewing life—and especially ourselves—with mistrust, trembling in fear at the prospect of the many mistakes we might make. If we cannot sense profound calm in our own hearts, we cannot experience life's abundance.

As long as we still believe that we have been abandoned by God because we were and are sinners, we cannot be free of a bad conscience.

Thus we cannot manifest freedom of heart in our life or experience the power of love. We cannot draw from life's abundance, and so we remain closed to divine creation.

To establish a connection to the divine, all we need to do is open the inner door and allow life to flow in us.

We need our bodies in order to do this. Not just our spiritual bodies, as we often believe, but also our material, physical bodies, which ground and anchor us.

Without them, we could not retain real life-energy.

If we can float and soar with our spirit it still does not mean that we are in intimate touch with the divine. True connection with the divine can only develop when we stand with both feet on the Earth. Only then can we serve as a pure pillar for profound exchange with the divine.

Oberweningen, January 26, 2004

We still believe that we are naïve know-nothings because we know much too little about the divine, because our cognitions about love are still too small, because we have too little information about life, because the heart's power remains relatively unexplored and we know much too little about it, etc.

One could say that we are a civilization obsessed with knowledge. We can never get enough of it.

The question is, are we doing all this because exploration is so deeply rooted in our nature? Are we doing it out of inner curiosity and pure interest, or are we avoiding something? We devote all of our attention and precious energy to collecting information and knowledge about life, and in the process we forget to live it.

We can know everything about a certain country, read all available books about it, know every little piece of it and its landscape from photos and maps, memorize every city, and study all the reports by archeologists, biologists, or geomancers, etc. until we understand them. We can even have the possibility to perceive the landscape through the map.

Plenty of knowledge and information are available, and we know everything we need to know. The only thing that is missing is direct, personal experience.

Only personal experience can supply us with the inner truth. Everything else is an illusion because it has nothing to do with our inner truth. Information that is not tuned in to our inner truth, that cannot really live within us, that cannot touch our hearts, remains empty and powerless.

In life, we busily gather knowledge about love, power of the heart, feelings and their effects, and so forth. We enjoy doing this; we feel virtuous and diligent. Nonetheless, we remain involved in planning our life's journey instead of actually setting out on it.

We are all the time on the verge of taking the step but do not dare to really do it. Because we are always preparing to immerse ourselves in life and commit ourselves to its flow, we are constantly tense and under pressure.

It's like having a perpetual case of travel nerves. We have decided to embark on the journey; we know exactly where we want to go. But we keep postponing our departure. Why do we do this? Because we suddenly discover that we don't have enough information about the country we plan to visit. Or perhaps we hope that the country will continue to be explored and the future will provide even better opportunities to learn more about it and prepare ourselves for the trip. Or, or, or.... There are always ifs and buts and too many lame excuses.

This may sound ironic, but if we think about it, we can see that we're doing exactly the same thing with our life. We are afraid of really living our life, so we always find new excuses for not doing it. We are fully aware that we are here in this life in order to actually make the journey and not to talk about it, think about it, analyze it, research it....

We are meant to explore life itself, not to plan life's journey indefinitely.

A house can look absolutely wonderful on the architect's plans, and yet we may not be able to live in it.

Our vision of life can be so wonderful, perfect, and complete, yet it remains an illusion as long as we are not ready and willing to live it.

Of course this does not mean yet that we ought to be living our vision right now in this moment. We should, however, dare to take the first step toward it. We should begin to implement it, or else it will remain nothing more than a plan, like a house on paper that cannot shelter us under its roof yet.

Of course it takes time, patience, energy, etc. to get to where we can "shape" and live our personal vision. But after a certain point, what we need is the decision and the courage to take the first step, so that we can make the transition from dream to reality, from planning to acting.

Life is given as a present to us to live!

Oberweningen, January 27, 2004

Why do we need such complicated religions and all the ecclesiastical systems that develop out of them, complex philosophies and theoretical explorations of life?

Life itself is essentially very plain and simple, very clear, and above all, very pure.

Why do we make it more complicated than it really is?

Is it because we believe that in this way we can give life the attention and accord it the importance it deserves? Or even that life becomes weightier or more valuable as a result? Do we think this is a way to demonstrate our own importance and to get our accomplishment noticed? Or do we perhaps make life difficult for ourselves simply because we enjoy playing the role of victim?

To repeat: *Life is not difficult and entangled; we make it hard for ourselves.*

Of course life is a riddle, and as such, it sometimes does look complicated.

We should know that life is not an unsolvable riddle, deliberately intended to make us lose our way, and we should not understand it as such. Instead, it is a challenge to us to finally open ourselves, to unfold our own power and beauty.

Let's not confuse challenge with provocation, because we should not see life as a provoker at all.

Life offers us diverse and extensive opportunities to learn and to practice. But it also gives us opportunities to decide for ourselves and does not require us to go in any particular direction.

Nor does it confront us on our way with lessons we are not yet ready to understand or with problems we cannot solve.

We are always required to take the next step, but we are not forced to do anything that is inappropriate to our path. We remain free: free of all kinds of projections, free of threats, free of severe punishments, and so on.

We can rest assured that regardless of what we have done or how hard we have tried to avoid new experiences, we will always have new opportunities to learn.

Still, it is a mistake and an illusion to imagine that making the path difficult for ourselves, really fighting our way through life and applying all our energy to the struggle, and truly suffering in the process, is necessary to show that we are giving life our energy and our attention—that only then can we really experience what life is and what it means to live.

Instead, in this way we will overlook beauty, sweetness, the nectar of life; and the maturity and depth that we want to present to life will get lost.

We do not increase either our rewards or our intrinsic value by seeing ourselves as the fighters and victims of a hard life.

On the contrary, the value of life will remain hidden from us, like an inaccessible treasure.

Life is simple. The only faith we really need to discover this treasure is faith of heart.

Oberweningen, January 28, 2004

If we look at ourselves and our life with total honesty for once, we will probably notice how many different masks we still need and how often we still follow empty clichés instead of listening to our heart.

It is not just that we are not ready to follow our heart. We even deny it; we attempt to hide it behind all kinds of junk; we voluntarily destroy it. We suppress every opportunity for our heart to shine, to finally reveal its power, and to unfold in its full light and glory.

The saddest thing is that in most situations in life we do this consciously.

What? We consciously suppress our own power? We don't allow it to expand?

This is where we are faced with a question that we really should answer honestly: Is it that we cannot allow the heart to expand, or that we do not want to?

As long as we are not ready, deep in our hearts, to find and actually to live our treasure, we cannot find it because we do not want to look for it. To search for it successfully requires a heartfelt desire to find it.

But first we need to realize that we are living without our treasure, or at least admit to ourselves that we are not manifesting it in our life and may not even want to.

As long as we think we are following our heart, our soul, and our task in life, we will not search, nor will we be ready to change anything in our life in order to find and manifest our treasure.

When it comes to such profound questions and decisions about life, masks are empty and valueless. Even if we invest them with power, they remain something of a farce.

But in spite of everything we are not ready to let go of them.

In spite of everything we outsmart ourselves.

And in spite of everything we choose to obey our masks instead of our inner truth.

Can we really not see this and finally be aware of it, or are we too proud to want to see it?

Pride often keeps us away from the new path that is already so close and waiting for us. Pride does not permit us to risk taking the first step. It takes away our courage to consider new opportunities. It can do all this because we let it. We give it the power and strength.

At this point, we again encounter the feeling of sin that has been so deeply imprinted on every cell in our body—first, because we were taught that we would be completely lost if we made mistakes or "sinned." Second, because if we did it anyway, we were supposed to feel ashamed and profoundly regretful, at the very least.

Instead of bolstering our courage and our strength to seek and find a new path.

Instead of trusting life and ourselves.

Instead of believing in our own hearts and thus providing new opportunities for ourselves.

So we remain victims of life and of our own "mistakes" and "flaws," and we feel sorry for ourselves. We make ourselves small and unimportant—simply out of pride, because we are not ready and willing to learn from the past in order to gain experience for the future.

Oberweningen, January 29, 2004

No one can help us develop faith if we do not believe in our own hearts. No one can build a holy temple for us if we are not ready to see ourselves as a temple of the divine.

We seek refuges and retreats in the religions, in outer temples, churches, and institutions. We forget that we are attempting to satisfy our hunger for heart's love and our longing for intimate connection. Fortunately for us, we cannot find these things in the outside world as long as we are not ready to draw on our inner resources, which is the only way we can be challenged to learn to rely on our own inner power and heart's love and above all to believe in our own inner truth.

We can only receive "outer" love when we reach for it out of abundance, not out of deprivation or need.

Reaching out from a position of abundance is the only way to preserve our independence of heart. It is the only way we can really receive what we long for, the only way we can accept and treasure the gifts we have received and bring them into life.

Faith begins and ends in our own heart. The only faith we can accept and pursue with all our being is the faith of our own heart.
Our treasure, our life's knowledge, and the anchor for our connection to the divine lie in our own heart. That is where the temple of the divine rises.

We can travel around the world looking for a suitable faith and religion; we can read all the books in the world seeking a solution; we can seek and even receive consolation from the hands of all human beings, but we will still not find the real support and steadfast pillar for our own temple of life.

The energy and stability needed for this temple of the divine can be found and activated only in our own heart.

The temple's foundation and structure can only be built up out of the inner power and faith of our heart.

We will grab for love forever in vain if we are not ready to reach for the eternity of our own heart and to draw unlimited heart's love from it.

We will search in vain for inner calm until we are finally ready to seek it in our own heart. Our heart is the only possible vessel for receiving the flow of the divine.

The heart cannot sin. The only thing we can regret in life is not enjoying it and thus not truly living it.

Even then, we need not feel remorse for long, because we are fortunate to be able to make a new decision at any moment and thus to "begin" life over again.

In this way we get life's rich gift in every moment.

Life is in our hands. We simply need to open the doors of our heart wide and allow light and love to flow and radiate again.
We simply need to open ourselves unconditionally and dare to enter into the exchange with life, with love, and with the heart's power.
Everything is ready and waiting. We simply need to take the step and rediscover the key of the heart, enliven it and use it, in order to open ourselves to life and love.

THE HEART IS THE ANCHOR, THE NAVEL OF OUR SPIRITUAL POWER.

Oberweningen, February 18, 2004

Photographs: From the Pyramids to Jerusalem

Giza plateau: Sphinx with the pyramids of Cheops and Chephren

Pyramids of Cheops and Chephren, Sphinx, Step Pyramid of Sakkara

Pyramid of Cheops, Sphinx, Step Pyramid of Sakkara

Sinai: oasis with Moses Springs

Sinai: oasis with Moses Springs

Sinai: St. Catherine's Monastery

Mount Sinai, valley of St. Catherine's Monastery

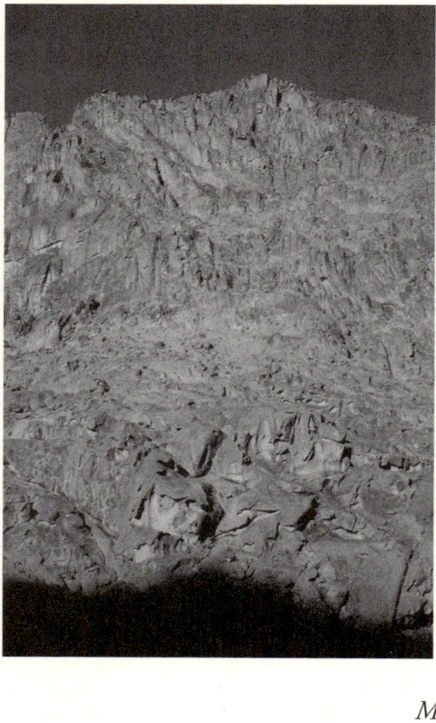

Mount Sinai

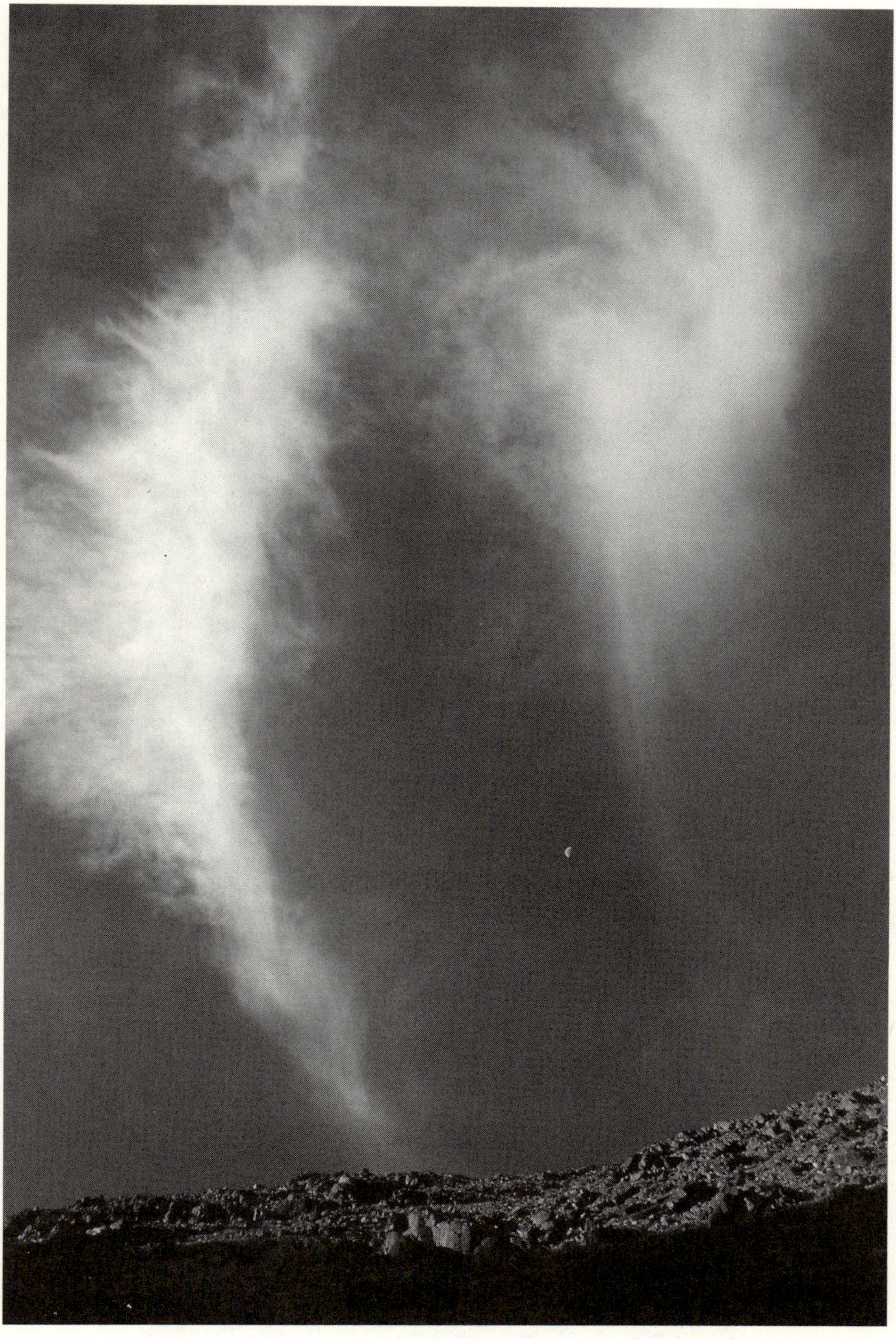

Mount Sinai

Elat: "Solomon's Pillars," Timna Park

Elat: "Solomon's Pillars," Timna Park

Red Sea

Avdat National Park

Dead Sea, Masada

Ein Gedi Nature Reserve, Dead Sea

Nahal David National Park

Nahal David National Park

Sea of Galilee, stone circle of Rujm el-Hiri

Stone circle of Rujm el-Hiri

Jerusalem: view of the city, Wailing Wall, Church of the Holy Sepulcher

Mount Zion

Dome of the Rock, Gate of Mercy

Mount of Olives

The Landscape around the Sea of Galilee as the World-Navel

What is the role played by this landscape, this geographical space? Why did such an important step in humankind's history take place exactly there?

The love and power of the heart that Jesus anchored is present and rooted everywhere. It cannot be bound to time and space and is in that way everywhere present.

But it is not equally intense all the time or in all places.

The area between the Dead Sea and the Sea of Galilee possesses a specific openness, a unique structure, and a clear vibration, which has allowed it to play a special role. This area is like a navel, the navel of the world.

In the human being, the navel represents the symbolic middle where everything is connected in the one, where spirit merges with matter. In the beginning of the our incarnation the navel connects us to the source and enables us in this phase to communicate concretely and directly with the world.

The navel is the "remnant" of the umbilical cord. It is like the footing of the bridge that makes our development possible, or—to put it better—the foundation on which we can build.

Symbolically speaking, we might say that the entire bridge is inherent in the navel. The bridge is multidimensional and therefore has the strength to connect everything within everything. It is a place of connection, thus also a turning point.

It is like a constantly rotating wheel that increases its energy exponentially.

Thus the navel is the place where everything is stored, including the potential for growth, and where energy for the primal process of development is awakened. It is the impulse that lays the basis for the beginning of life, the foundation of life's structure.

The location of the navel also symbolizes the first step toward self-reliance. It presents the opportunity to embody everything and to anchor the spirit in matter. And it also represents the bridge that does the anchoring.

Thinking of the landscape of Galilee as the world-navel helps us imagine its role and function.

This space has the energy, potential, and openness to serve as a bridge for the spiritual world and the divine to manifest very concretely in material form. In this landscape, the foundation of life could be built. It was the impulse that was so clear here and could make the necessary energy available.

This is what made it possible for the bridge—the bridge that was like an umbilical cord—to be constructed.

Šempas, January 2, 2004

This umbilical cord made it possible to incorporate the divine into matter, into the concrete, and anchor it there. The result was an enormous release of faith-energy, which supported this development.

The intensity, power and clarity of the local landscape and the temporal constellation made it possible for divine and spiritual nourishment to be greatly enhanced and intensified. It became so close, so dense, and so clearly present that the basis of faith could develop, and the divine could manifest in physical form.

Just as at birth, also in the landscape: only the basis should remain in the form of the navel, not as the entire umbilical cord.

In the beginning, enthusiasm and euphoria preserved the bridge so the intensity could not get lost. Faith was consciously maintained. As fear of losing the intensity of the divine present increased, this pure enthusiasm gradually hardened into rigidity.

Out of the greed for power that developed through this process, the umbilical cord was never cut and never abandoned. That symbolic step toward self-reliance was never taken.

The faith and the religions that originated in this area were clearly bound to the landscape, the people, and the time. Instead of making the transition to independent development, the process solidified.

No umbilical cord can persist forever without exhausting the source it draws upon.

Instead of serving as an anchoring pillar, the landscape itself was used as the source.

Freedom was not possible anymore.

The bridge itself could not survive this brutal rigidification. The source is exhausted.

The openness and intensity of the landscape burned out. The true core was destroyed, and the intensity of the connection was no longer possible. What remained are ossified religions still clinging to an umbilical cord that is long since dead.

The tragic euphoria of faith and the grievous fight for religious authority shrouded everything in confusion instead of preserving the navel of the world. To experience the energy of the center, we should dig for it deep beneath the murk of this chaos.

The function of the navel is still present.

Information, life-energy, and heart's love are all still securely anchored in the landscape. They have been used and often misused, but they have not been uprooted, and so the real, primal basis is still alive.

In our time, spiritual intensity, divine presence, heart's love and life-energy are once again condensing and intensifying, almost pressing upon us. A new opportunity to anchor the divine more concretely seems to be trying to take root, but this time without the power and help of a specific landscape and concrete individuals.

We humans have come so far that we could be capable of being the bridge ourselves.

Because of the rigidity of religions, because the force behind them is not ready to let go, and above all because fear still governs our connection to the divine, pressure on the navel, the middle, is intensifying.

This landscape still occupies the central position and thus serves the function of the navel.

It is still meant to be an anchor, a pillar, an opening that enables pure, clear divine power to take root everywhere.

This is the landscape that provides the energy and the opportunity to anchor and support this important impulse. This impulse is needed for our development and connection, because we too are part of the whole.

This sounds almost impossible, but unfortunately this is the reality of the situation, although we might prefer not to believe it. This landscape is being pressured very consciously. It is being cloaked in suffering, hate, and separation to prevent it from offering the openness that is so desperately needed.

It cannot support the step that we are waiting for and are ready to take. It also cannot serve as the pillar for a new connection.

Thus the process is held up and the power and might of churches and religions persist and are artificially maintained.

The next step is being blocked, and with it development!

Šempas, January 3, 2004

This landscape presents a central opening supported by a very strong vital-energetic structure. As the world-navel, this geographical area is also a unity, a microcosm of the whole, the core where the essence is stored. It is the foundation that still carries information within it.

Such a strong opening needs support, and one of its primary supports consists of two pyramids of light, one pointing up and the other down.

They represent the connection and merger of the divine with the material, the cosmos with the earth, the vertical with the horizontal, the male with the female, the inner with the outer.

This is the archetypal pattern and plan for anchoring the divine spirit and connecting it with creation.

It is the navel, the basis of the impulse for exchange.

This archetypical principle and the structure that arises from it appear everywhere, repeatedly, and continue to be active. This structure is the fundamental impulse and thus also the basis.

It manifests in the landscape, it is active in us humans, it is present in the smallest of plants, it is found in crystals, it is seen in the stars, and so forth.

Wherever there is life, this structure is present and active in the background.

This double connection supports and constantly renews the impulse of life and makes an ongoing cycle possible at all.

Through this constant connection, the flow of life develops.

This structure with its two pyramids is like a constantly turning wheel. It is an ongoing process engaged in eternal development.

However, through the process of induration that was manifested in fixed, restrictive religions, this mobile system has been paralyzed and brought to a standstill. Everything has been held back and frozen at a certain stage in the process.

This was a result of fear of losing the openness that had been won, the clarity that was present, the profound connection with the divine. It was an attempt to bring the process to a halt, to apply the brakes to time and especially to development. Unfortunately, it later became primarily an attempt to preserve the power and dominance that had been established.

The admiration and enthusiasm for concrete manifestations of power and of the divine became so pronounced that we failed to notice we were clinging too tightly to the rigid structure of the churches and religions and impressing our burden on the underlying etheric structure. This pressure blocked that entire structure and turned it to stone.

Šempas, January 7, 2004

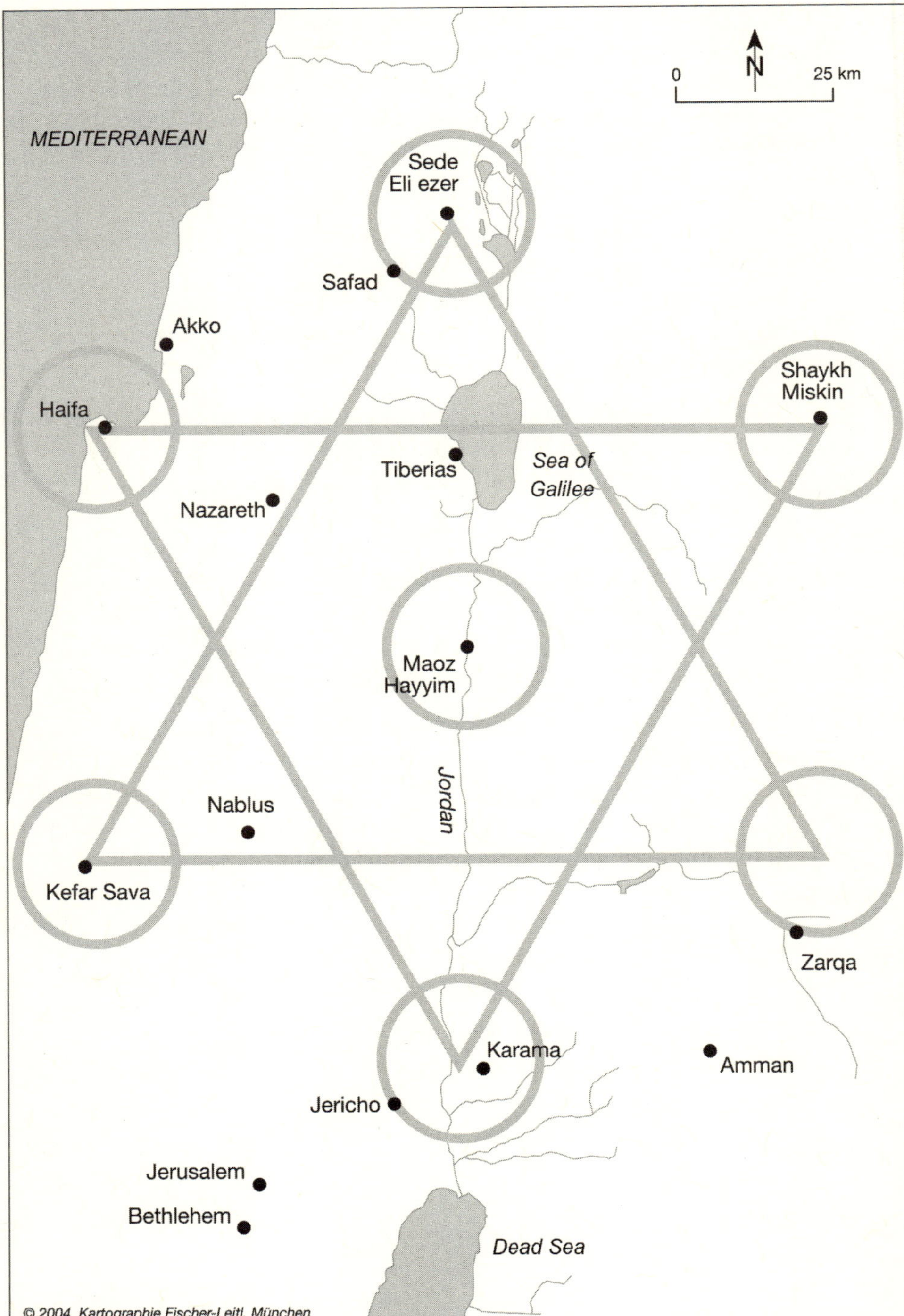

0
N
25 km
MEDITERRANEAN
Sede
Eli ezer
Safad
Akko
Haifa
Shaykh
Miskin
Tiberias
Sea of
Galilee
Nazareth
Maoz
Hayyim
Jordan
Nablus
Kefar Sava
Zarqa
Karama
Amman
Jericho
Jerusalem
Bethlehem
Dead Sea
© 2004, Kartographie Fischer-Leitl, München

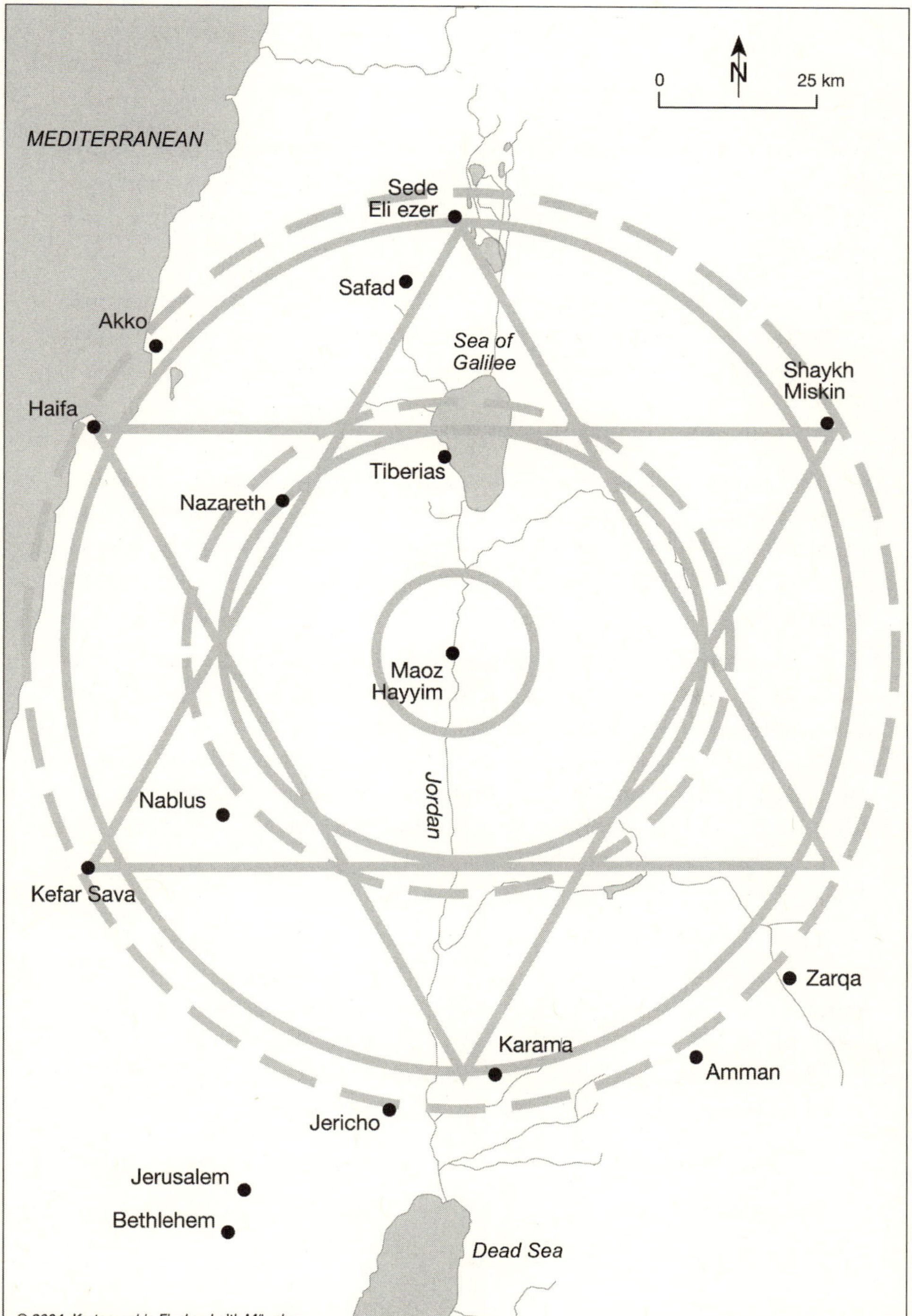
MEDITERRANEAN
0
N
25 km
Sede
Eli ezer
Safad
Akko
Sea of
Galilee
Shaykh
Miskin
Haifa
Tiberias
Nazareth
Maoz
Hayyim
Jordan
Nablus
Kefar Sava
Zarqa
Karama
Amman
Jericho
Jerusalem
Bethlehem
Dead Sea
© 2004, Kartographie Fischer-Leitl, München

Flow, current became impossible, and the underlying principle of the divine, the essence of this structure, rigidified. The constantly developing and moving wheel of life was forced to a stop in order to obstruct and paralyze development.

The power of the system was usurped and used against its own nature. Energy that was created to serve and be responsible for constant growth, eternal development and the endless flow of life was now used to prevent them or slow them down.

It was forced to destroy its own core.

Without clinging to this system again, but simply to get a better idea of it, let's consider the concrete places, even better to say, landscape-spaces. It is important to emphasize again that the "navel" of this landscape is only one possible manifestation of this universal principle. It is not the only one that can save us all.

As already mentioned, the structure consists of two pyramids: six "cornerstones" in the form of landscape-spaces, the peaks of the two pyramids, and a central column running through the peaks.

The resulting structure includes nine energetic spaces—six on the horizontal plane, two in the vertical dimension, and one connecting the two dimensions. All this is only the framework of the whole system, because all of the landscape spaces together form a single light-body, a closed sphere of light.

This means that the vertical is connected with the horizontal, above is linked to below, left and right are inseparable in this system, the Earth is connected to the Cosmos and spirit is interwoven with matter....

Everything that exists is one with all and in all. Separation is no longer possible.

Oberweningen, January 17, 2004

If we continue to observe these two pyramidal structures, we discover three spheres, indicated by three circles.

The first sphere is the inner space with the central axis running through it. It encircles not just the pillar but the entire space. In this way it is not just a two-dimensional circle but a multidimensional, ball-shaped sphere.

The space of the second sphere ends at the outline we get when we connect the points where the legs of the pyramids intersect.

The outermost space is formed by the circle connecting the points of the triangles. All three circular spaces should be seen as spherical.

This system incorporates all of the directions; all except the east-west line run through two corners of the pyramids. This exception is not a mistake. Rather, it points to the important role of this direction in the cycle of life and in faith itself. Namely, it indicates the path or cycle of life, which is fluid rather than fixed or direct. It defines (but does not pin down) rising and setting, birth and death, growth and change, and the emergence and transformation of form and dimensions.

These are indicated by the openings formed by the two legs of the pyramid in the east-west direction. Like two open doors, they invite us into the cycle of life.

All of the direction lines cross the axis in the center, creating the vertical dimension and connecting the entire universe in the core.

The vertical space of the pyramids and of the system as a whole is also subdivided into several spherical layers.

The lowest layer begins on a level with the peak of the lower pyramid and encompasses all the space to within approximately one hundred meters of the Earth's surface, where the middle layer begins.

This is where the bases of the pyramids and all their corners and intersection points lie.

The upper sphere begins a hundred meters above the surface and extends to the tip of the upper pyramid.

The middle layer plays the connecting role, since it is where the two basic streams of energy flow together.

We can imagine this happening in the form of two spirals, one flowing upward from the tip of the lower pyramid and the other downward from the upper peak. The spirals are best imagined as two flowing vortices filling the entire interior of the pyramids.

On the level of the bases of the two pyramids, these two streams converge and unite, and some of their interwoven energy spreads throughout the whole surrounding area, while the rest flows on in the original directions.

These two streams are given additional support by the central axis. This pillar maintains the connection that develops as the result of the exchange between the two streams.

In this respect, the pillar is similar to our spine. It is not itself the connection and does not really uphold it, but it does make the connection possible and provide solidity. Its concentrated, condensed energy provides an opportunity for intensive exchange and communication between different dimensions.

Oberweningen, January 17, 2004

This whole system is centered, anchored, and stabilized by the axis and its landscape-space. As a result of the energy flowing in it, the pillar's space is constantly moving and adapting.

It is the place where everything flows together: where the two spiral streams from the peaks of the pyramids interweave to form the vertical, where the qualities of all the directions cross and flow into each other. The space of the axis is also where the lines coming from all the corners of the pyramids connect. These lines are clearly perceptible also in the landscape as energy lines.

When we connect these lines with the central spherical space, we get a sunlike form with the concentration in the middle and eight concentric rays. The two vertical rays are part of the axis and support the vertical connection, while the other six rays enable energetic exchange on the horizontal plane.

These lines are actually more like channels that make an exchange process possible because energy flows through them in both directions.

The entire description of the system of pyramids deals with three-dimensional landscape-spaces—not just isolated points but the spheres or spherical spaces determined by these points.

It is a system that is constantly rotating and moving and therefore involved in an eternal process of transformation.

The whole system is like a buoy that floats on the water, adjusts itself to conditions in the water, on the surface, in the surroundings, and in the air, and in this way constantly repositions itself.

Nothing is fixed or immobile. From moment to moment, the energy, flow-through, and qualities are changing from what they were before.

The two pyramids can be characterized as the male and female principles, negative and positive, yin and yang. We can describe the upper pyramid as yang and the lower one as yin.

The pyramids are connected not only by the spiral flow described above but also by a kind of breathing or, even better, a pulsation that develops between these two poles. The interplay between these two energetic bodies or landscape-spaces is unending.

Now we can attempt to pinpoint these two spherical bodies in the landscape itself.

First, the three corners of the lower pyramid: the first is located near Haifa (along the coast north of Tel Aviv), the second in the landscape sphere of Shaykh Miskin in Jordan (east of the Sea of Galilee) and the third just west of Karama (north of the Dead Sea).

The three corners of the upper pyramid: the first is located in the landscape space northeast of Safad (near Sede Eli'ezer, north of the Sea of Galilee), the second north of Zarqa (in Jordan, northeast of Amman), and the third near Kafar Sava (east of Herzliya or northeast of Tel Aviv). The length of each edge of the pyramids is about one hundred and ten kilometers.

Places are given only for the sake of orientation. Each corner marks an entire energetic sphere of its own with a diameter of fifteen to twenty-two kilometers.

The middle of the whole system is located in the landscape space around Maoz Hayim.

Oberweningen, January 24, 2004

If we forget and erase all fixed forms for a brief moment, what stays is the essence of life and creation.

The pyramidal system described here is an important bearer of such power. Through its strong but subtle structure the elemental impulse of life is maintained here in the form of energy. It feels as if everything that exists, lives, and pulsates meets here in one single point, one single cell, one single system.

The firm and stable structure grounds and sustains, and makes possible the manifestation of a complete organ.

These two pyramids, one positioned so exactly above the other, function like an amplifier of purest energy. They amplify not only the pure energy that can and does flow through here but also (and to an even greater extent) the impulse that plays such an important role in the creation of life.

This is the essence of life, the fundamental creative power. It is the power religions call the creator or God the Creator. It is the impulse that can stimulate life. Its emanation and effects are so concrete and clear that all possible forms of life can emerge from it.

This energetic system is a framework for the power that it anchors. Although humans have used it to amplify energy on behalf of humankind, the structure was not created by human deeds and history. It has always existed.

The spherical space that develops through the concentrated energy and intensified impulse influences the shape of this system, which is anchored in the landscape. This shape enables the impulse to become more concrete and thus clearer in its effects. The form itself causes life and all its parts to separate and fall apart into fragments, individual parts, and into primal cells of life. This affords them a new opportunity to rearrange themselves, reconnect, and find themselves anew.

This is a process of transformation in which solid form first disappears for a moment as it submits to the effects of transformation, so that it can be composed anew and find, with increased power, a new and different form for its expression.

This is in fact the very elementary formula of life: "*You are born out of the impulse of creation so that you may follow the path of transformation and ultimately return to the impulse of creation with new experiences."*

This energetic structure supports, stimulates, and even demands this process of transformation in every instant of eternity.

Life is nothing fixed. This means that the process, the formula of life is present and active at every moment in every living thing, every human being, every landscape....

What is reflected in the system that lies before us is the game of life. This system is reflected in all forms of life and thus it is reflected in each of us.

Oberweningen, January 27, 2004

Our bodies are constructed according to this system. Or, to put it differently, we can also recognize this system in the human body. Through our existence, we connect Earth and Cosmos, we connect vertical and horizontal, we live female and male simultaneously and above all, we embody the impulse of life.

We are also a pillar that makes a variety of connections possible and in which different aspects flow together to merge in the middle.

The center is the heart and the connecting energy is the power of the heart.

If we keep all this in mind, we will be better able to understand why this system played such an important role in humankind's history and why we can see this particular landscape as a navel.

What we see reflected before our eyes in this system is the image of life itself. We see roots in which we can recognize ourselves, the basis from which the impulse is drawn repeatedly. It is the form that we anchor and recognize in our own existence, our own life, at every step we take.

The spirit is anchored in matter, and so matter can also expand into spiritual spheres. The Earth is reflected in the cosmos, and so the cosmos can also descend into the Earth.

What is above is also below, and what is inside is outside at the same time.

The giver is at the same time a receiver, for the impulse is simultaneously given and received.

Boundaries, limitations, and separations have no place among the roots of life, and therefore they have no power in this system.

This is exactly why it is so sad that we have used—and still use—this unlimited, connecting power to establish boundaries and to restrict ourselves, our surroundings, and even other people.

The power that is so clearly and intensely present in this system can be compared to the Big Bang. This is the moment when everything that exists connects and in which the total potential of life-energy "crushes" together to merge again.

It is the point where everything is so clearly present and such intense movement emerges that we feel as if everything is standing still. It is like a nought point, a point of origin where everything is simultaneously standing still and moving vigorously.

This is the moment when moving calm and still motion develop.

Oberweningen, April 6, 2004

From our own incarnation process, at least, we are all familiar with this moment of unconditional and unbounded accord, the feeling of being one with everything and in everything, of being an expression of the creation of life.

It is the same enormous concentration and intensity as in the moment when the soul takes root in matter and in the body and the process of real incarnation begins. This is the instant of "being one with everything."

Great openness develops simultaneously with great density and constriction, which also makes it possible for the entire creative energy of life to manifest and connect.

This is the moment of peace; this is the power of calm.

This is the state we are searching for, the condition we long for so dearly: to sense the presence of the divine and of all creation within us, to carry it and *be* it; to achieve inner calm that allows us to go with the flow of life unconditionally, without fear and with all our power. This is the centered power of calm, which keeps us in balance in life and gives us steadiness.

This specific energy and the inner state that results from it are anchored and rooted by the system described above. They are present with enormous intensity in the landscape around the Sea of Galilee.

The energetic system in this geographical area is not the only system that takes this form. The double pyramid appears frequently in the landscape, supporting the concrete anchoring of this energy wherever it appears. But the system around the Sea of Galilee can be seen as the mother system, the basis, the energetic lighthouse that provides orientation and to which all other such systems are attuned.

Only in this particular space is the impulse present in the landscape with such unique intensity, so close and so dense that it is almost tangible.

The impulse of peace, the power of connection, the basis of universal reconciliation, the all-encompassing power of the heart, the creative power of life are so concentrated, centered, and intensified here in this landscape. Yet this is precisely where deeply cutting boundaries are built, where insoluble misunderstandings are inflamed, leading to enmity, where endless wars are waged and bloody attempts are carried out.

How is this possible, and why do we need it?

Have we humans still not learned enough from the constant wars we wage? Is our desire for inner peace still not stronger than greed for justification and dominance?

When we consider the situation in this landscape and in the world as a whole, it becomes clear to us that we really do still need this outer mirror, unfortunate as it may be.

Even though we experience the enormous power of the Big Bang in the process of incarnation, even though our deeper being longs for peace and connection, we still lack inner peace.

We experience internal conflict on a daily basis, wage war within ourselves, and pour our energy into these struggles. We cannot make peace between the individual parts and aspects of ourselves. By sabotaging our own power, we experience constant assassinations within ourselves.

How then can we expect the world around us to reflect anything different? Unfortunately, it cannot be different.

As long as we are not ready to make peace with and within ourselves to enable us to radiate the power of calm, the power of the heart, the power of Christ, the power of the divine, and above all to *live* it, we cannot expect to experience peace on Earth

The landscape system described above cannot function in full force because it mirrors each one of us. Specifically, it reflects how we handle our own power, our own heart, and our own center. It reflects the extent to which we are receptive and ready to enter into connection.

The "search" for peace, and thus also the peace process, begins in us.

This is why we need not feel helpless in view of the situation in this land. At the same time we should not imagine that unrest and war there are far away and have nothing to do with us.

By translating outer actions and situations into inner terms, we can understand the processes taking place within ourselves. We can look within for the assassins who pull the ground from under our feet. We can redeem them and transform them and stop feeding them with our power.

It is our decision in which direction we send our power, to direct our attention and bestow our energy, our decision what to support with our existence, our presence.

What we need first is the decision. Only then can the path of life begin.

Oberweningen, April 8, 2004